FAKE SALVATION
in MODERN GNOSTIC AMERICA

FAKE SALVATION
in **MODERN GNOSTIC AMERICA**

CHRISTOPHER RAOUL CARRANZA

WIPF & STOCK · Eugene, Oregon

FAKE SALVATION IN MODERN GNOSTIC AMERICA

Copyright © 2025 Christopher Raoul Carranza. All rights reserved. Except for brief quotations in critical publications or reviews, no part of this book may be reproduced in any manner without prior written permission from the publisher. Write: Permissions, Wipf and Stock Publishers, 199 W. 8th Ave., Suite 3, Eugene, OR 97401.

Wipf & Stock
An Imprint of Wipf and Stock Publishers
199 W. 8th Ave., Suite 3
Eugene, OR 97401

www.wipfandstock.com

PAPERBACK ISBN: 979-8-3852-5015-8
HARDCOVER ISBN: 979-8-3852-5016-5
EBOOK ISBN: 979-8-3852-5017-2

VERSION NUMBER 071425

All Scripture quotations unless otherwise marked are taken from The Holy Bible, New International Version®, NIV®. Copyright © 1973, 1978, 1984, 2011 by Biblica, Inc. Used with permission of Zondervan. All rights reserved worldwide. www.zondervan.com.

Scripture quotations marked (KJV) are from The Authorized (King James) Version. Rights in the Authorized Version in the United Kingdom are vested in the Crown. Reproduced by permission of the Crown's patentee, Cambridge University Press.

CONTENTS

INTRODUCTION | vii

CHAPTER 1
ANCIENT GNOSTICISM | 1

CHAPTER 2
GNOSTIC AMERICA | 11

CHAPTER 3
LORD, LORD | 19

CHAPTER 4
PAINTED INTO A CORNER: DISPENSATIONALISM | 33

CHAPTER 5
SHOW ME A PICTURE | 54

CHAPTER 6
IGNORING THE CONTRADICTIONS | 75

CHAPTER 7
HOW DID WE GET HERE? | 93

CHAPTER 8
UNACCEPTABLE DIVERGENCE | 117

BIBLIOGRAPHY | 143

INTRODUCTION

"Timing is everything." Fortunately, the time for this book's publication has finally arrived. Throughout history, a common thread emerges: ideas gain acceptance only when their time is right—not before.

For half a century, I, along with others, have been passionately criticizing dispensationalist pastors and mainstream American churches for promoting a distorted version of salvation. Popular easy-believism has led countless individuals to feel a false sense of assurance regarding their eternal redemption. In reality, they were only being offered a deceptive illusion—a fake guarantee of salvation that carries no weight with God.

Dispensationalism, a system that only arose in the early nineteenth century, is a contemporary version of a gnostic gospel that has existed for nearly two millennia. The sole purpose of all forms of Gnosticism, whether from ancient times or modern, is to offer individuals a sense of certainty and assurance about their personal salvation. This singular focus often overshadows the need for an honest and thorough interpretation of scriptural texts. In truth, the precision of the Bible often takes a back seat, exemplified by the intentional creation of false gnostic books in the second century. This highlights a broader trend that favors personal enlightenment over adherence to strict theological accuracy. The end justifies the means in this belief system, where creating a gnostic "omelet" is preemptory, even if it requires breaking a few scriptural "eggs" along the way.

But suddenly, the very people who had dogmatically defended Protestant easy-believism and the two-hundred-year-old dispensational gospel and spent their entire careers awarding unconditional salvation over the airwaves and at church and stadium altar calls are themselves adding contradictory conditions to their teachings. Have they finally come to understand the profound biblical truths that critics have been confronting them with for decades? No.

INTRODUCTION

It appears that by borrowing the dispensational foundational teachings of *"Behavior doesn't matter," Christ's finished work on the cross, the guarantees in 1 John 5:13, sinner's prayer pseudo-conversion,* and *the awarding of instantaneous irrevocable salvation,* the homosexual community has found a cure for the chronic blindness of mainstream Protestantism and dispensationalism. However, it's only a partial miracle; they can now see clearly when looking outward, but their vision fails them again when they turn to face a mirror.

Many mainstream pastors are now rushing to reassess and reshape core beliefs and doctrines that were once regarded as foundational and unquestionably biblical. However, untangling this rigid, two-hundred-year-old dispensational knot requires the flawed memory of individuals willing to forget everything they've been taught. These people are leaving with the pastor while others, who question whether they should now trust a pastor who has just admitted that everything he taught them for decades was a lie, are staying. This situation highlights how shifts in external culture and society can force hardened, duplicitous individuals to finally succumb to truth.

More pointedly, the homosexual revolution's intrusion into the church has caused dispensationalists to break into the sealed, easy-believism vault, only to discover that it has been bankrupt all along. Interestingly, there must be a spiritual vault elsewhere that they can draw from to grant salvation to heterosexual individuals they've never met. Otherwise, all unconditional salvation allegedly promised through airwaves, altar calls, and stadium events would have ended, which it hasn't.

In an apparent non sequitur, dispensationalism and modern Protestantism are still routinely engaged in the casual act of granting salvation over the radio, through TV ministries, and during church altar calls. Unbeknownst to them, they are employing a modified version of the gnostic script—"Behavior doesn't matter," Christ's finished work on the cross, the guarantees in 1 John 5:13, sinner's prayer pseudo-conversion, and the awarding of instantaneous irrevocable salvation—for heterosexual parishioners, while at the same time condemning its use for homosexual parishioners.

I'm certainly not advocating for homosexual inclusion in the church, but merely pointing out the obvious. It would seem that the "Behavior doesn't matter" / "Christ's finished work on the cross" dispensational gospel would apply to all deviant sexual behaviors or no deviant sexual behaviors.

INTRODUCTION

Modifying the "Cheap Grace" gospel so that it still applies to heterosexuals but excludes homosexuals demands a careful and intentional form of deceit.

The recent fracturing of churches over this contentious issue presents a fascinating dynamic. In numerous instances, those who choose to depart due to homosexual acceptance are actually in the minority. The roots of this divide can largely be traced back to the theological frameworks of dispensationalism and contemporary Protestantism, which must shoulder the responsibility for the current situation.

Those who remain within the congregations have held on to the notion of easy-believism, accepting that moral behavior is irrelevant, a concept deeply ingrained in their dispensational, modern Protestant upbringing. Most of them came to Christ through this unconditional approach, embracing the idea of "Christ's finished work," and that "none of our own works can be added to it." They are convinced of their salvation because they've been repeatedly and undeniably taught that 1 John 5:13 applies to every member of their church, including the homosexual members.

Members of the congregation who are leaving grapple with the pastor's recent teachings, which assert that his previous decades of preaching on unconditional salvation were fundamentally misguided. The pastor now claims that his altar calls and the sinner's prayer conversions—a cornerstone of their faith journey—were mere illusions, lacking actual substance as they no longer apply to the people who stayed behind. Despite this drastic change, he insists that the promise of guaranteed salvation somehow still applies specifically to each individual who leaves with him.

Yes, in years past, it was a comprehensive initiative encompassing the entire church, a promise the pastor made with unwavering conviction and certainty. Yet, in the present, it no longer applies to those congregants who chose to remain behind. The pastor's unique interpretation of "irrevocable salvation" suddenly seems to lose its permanence, as those who stayed behind have had their "irrevocable salvation" revoked.

In the following pages, I intend to illustrate how the entirety of American Protestantism has gradually degenerated into a more nuanced and insidious manifestation of the already distorted nineteenth-century American religious mindset. What began as a slow fall to the bottom—a "Christianity" that prioritized pleasing the masses and catering to their desires for a more palatable form of faith—turned into a landslide. This shift was triggered by the remarkable wealth and materialistic values that emerged in

INTRODUCTION

the aftermath of World War II, further intensified by the significant cultural transformations brought about by the sexual revolution.

The race to the bottom accelerated at a maddening pace during "the religious crisis of the 1960s"[1] until finally, by 2025, virtually all of American Christianity had devolved entirely into modern Gnosticism—which will be explained in chapter 2. When examining the diverse expressions of Gnosticism—an ancient belief system that stems from the Greek word meaning "to know"—one can trace its roots from the second century and observe its evolution through the ages leading up to the present. A consistent theme emerges across its various forms: the promise of guaranteed salvation for those who embrace its teachings.

One of the challenges this book faces is that, unlike in other fields, there are few fixed definitions when debating religious matters. That's because theological discussions rely on Scripture, and every appeal to Scripture relies on the interpretation of that Scripture the listener chooses to embrace. My conversations with Jehovah's Witnesses and their leadership highlighted this point distinctly: if their leaders insist that black means white, and members accept this "doublespeak," any scriptural argument effectively falls flat.

For that reason and others, I will, at times, use the Jehovah's Witnesses as a striking example of my premise, as their distinct brand of fake salvation and post-Christian Gnosticism is blatant and easily recognizable to almost anyone. After we find common ground on easily recognizable aspects, I believe those open to seeing it will also notice similar, albeit subtler, manifestations of the same premise within their own Protestant churches. These subtler variations might unfold in sermons, community practices, or even in how congregants engage with one another, revealing previously unrecognized manifestations of the premise.

I sincerely hope that even those who are in the habit of deliberately turning a blind eye and are skilled at sidestepping any uncomfortable truth will at least pause for a moment to consider the possibility that there may be a small nugget of truth in the premise that pertains to their church. May God guide your understanding as you read, and may he rein me in and guide me as I write.

---

1. See Hugh McLeod's book by the same name: McLeod, *Religious Crisis of the 1960s*.

CHAPTER 1

ANCIENT GNOSTICISM

For over fifteen centuries, the essence of gnostic beliefs has been shrouded in contradiction and mystery. This obscurity stems primarily from the systematic destruction of much of their literature by early Christian factions, who sought to suppress these alternative spiritual teachings. Compounding this issue, much of what we knew about their beliefs came from the accounts of those who opposed them, painting a skewed perspective that further distorted our understanding of them. Individuals had been free to blend their personal beliefs with various interpretations of Gnosticism. One outcome of this blending was a renewed interest in a more secular and philosophical form of Gnosticism during the early twentieth century, which attracted notable figures such as the famous psychologist Carl Jung. However, their most enduring legacy is probably their successful church growth formula, which played on human pride, exclusivity, elitism, the authority of one's own spiritual self-assessment, and eternal guarantees, which has been successfully employed down through the millennia and lives on today.

The fog of uncertainty that had enveloped the gnostics began to lift somewhat in 1945 with the discovery of the Nag Hammadi library in Egypt. By chance, a local farmer discovered a buried, sealed jar containing multiple codices believed to have been written during the third or fourth centuries. Contained within the codices were over fifty different compositions, all written in the Coptic language. This find turned out to be a treasure trove of early gnostic writings explaining some of their authentic beliefs and tenets. However, since it was written for the gnostic believers themselves, many of the finer points of their theology were left out because it was assumed that the faithful already knew the basics. Moreover, as explained in the documentary series *Ancient Roads from Christ to Constantine*, it's very difficult to define Gnosticism because of all its various groups, diverse fragmentations, and independent beliefs. When asked what the gnostics believed, Dr. Rebecca Lyman hit the nail on the head when she replied, "That's a highly contested question. . . . You might see these as people in these communities that didn't necessarily have strict boundaries, doing different exegesis on the Bible stories and writing different accounts."[1]

Christian Gnosticism, a movement with diverse biblical accounts, emerged in various forms in the second century AD.[2] While Marcion headed one prominent faction, the most significant and lasting branch of Gnosticism was led by Valentinus. His theology was originally in line with apostolic Christianity. So much so that in AD 136, he found himself in the esteemed position of being a candidate for the prominent role of bishop of Rome, but the Church of Rome ultimately turned down his candidacy, leaving his dreams of leading one of Christendom's most prominent communities unrealized. He was further humiliated by being excommunicated. After this embarrassment, his theology took a radical turn, and he used his brilliant mind and biblical expertise to convince large sections of the Eastern Roman Empire that Gnosticism was the true Christianity of the apostles.

The populace was very receptive to the central message of Gnosticism, and the movement grew like wildfire. The name "gnostic" means "the knowledgeable ones." Using the age-old psychological ploys of flattery, exceptionalism, and manipulative crowd-pleasing escapism, he promised every one of his listeners salvation by knowledge. By merely being present in his audience, committing to groupthink, and accepting his statements as authoritative—mainly because they were hearing exactly what they wished to hear—their salvation was irrevocably guaranteed.

Valentinus, a charismatic orator, easily convinced the throngs who were attracted to him wherever he journeyed that they were a chosen group, born with the divine spark, and that they had exclusive possession of secret knowledge. In light of this, the gnostics felt entitled to take extreme liberties in propagating their spiritually discerned truths. They wrote books

---

1. Lyman in Galan, "Apocalypse to Heresies," 3:14.

2. For further reading on the history summarized here, see Carranza, *Battle for the Divinity*.

interfused with their vocabulary and dogma, but in the style of genuine apostolic writings, and then falsely ascribed to them some weighty New Testament names. Most of their writings were penned much later than the volumes that would become the current twenty-seven New Testament books. Among their pseudepigraphal books are titles such as the Gospel of Mary Magdalene, the Gospel of Judas, the Prayer of the Apostle Paul, the Secret Book of James, the Gospel of Thomas, the Gospel of Philip, the Apocalypse of Paul, the Apocalypse of James, the Gospel of Truth, the Acts of Peter and the Twelve Apostles, and the Letter of Peter to Philip—as well as many other fabricated writings endorsing their theology.

The motivation behind creating these various books captures the core essence of Gnosticism, both in the past two millennia and in our present day: "The Gnostic texts were written so that the Gnostics could know [the certainty of] their own salvation."[3]

That was the purpose of the entire system. Valentinus recognized the necessity of capturing the attention of carnal, self-centered Roman-world hedonists. The ancient Roman world provided an unparalleled environment for individuals seeking the freedom to engage in open and unrestrained hedonism. The fact that about one-third of the population were slaves allowed the remaining two-thirds who weren't slaves more leisure time for self-indulgence.

Valentinus did not begin his pitch by discussing the New Testament essentials of self-denial, self-sacrifice, and a wholehearted commitment to serving God. He left that kind of talk to the followers of Jesus' apostles, the "proto-orthodox," which is the term used for the group that would eventually win out and become orthodox Christianity. Instead, Valentinus immediately recognized and focused on the totality of their core spiritual concerns: What's in it for me? And what was in it for them was immediate salvation, guaranteed and irrevocable.

Valentinus "proved" that they were saved using legitimate writings from Paul, only later pushing his own fabricated books to further convince them of their elitism. Valentinus highlighted the verses where Paul mentioned knowledge and then convinced his listeners that Paul was speaking to them personally and that the implications of those verses powerfully endorsed and praised the gnostics. Paul used the words *knowledge* and *know* in many verses, and Valentinus cleverly personalized and took advantage of those particular Scriptures, including many like the ones below:

3. Lee, *Against the Protestant Gnostics*, 4.

- Rom 10:2: "Their [enemies'] zeal is not based on knowledge." (Implying that those who opposed them were scripturally ignorant.)
- Rom 11:33: "Oh, the depth of the riches of wisdom and knowledge . . ." (Inflating their intellectual pride by informing them that the gnostics alone were the only repository of Christian understanding.)
- Rom 15:14: "You yourselves are full of goodness, filled with knowledge and competent to instruct one another." (Further stoking their pride by also attributing to them the quality of goodness.)
- 1 Cor 1:5: "For in him you have been enriched in every way—with all kinds of speech and with all knowledge." (Assuring them that only the gnostics have the words of truth.)
- 1 Cor 8:7: "But not everyone possesses this knowledge." (The continued emphasis on the "us versus them" mentality, which is always a fundamental aspect of Gnosticism.)
- 1 Cor 12:8: "To one there is given through the spirit a message of wisdom, to another a message of knowledge by means of the same spirit." (Valentinus confirmed for them that everything he was saying and guaranteeing came directly from God's Spirit, not from himself.)
- 2 Cor 2:14: "[God] uses us to spread the aroma of the knowledge." (We, the gnostics, are the only true teachers of God's word and the only Christians whom God uses in proselytizing. Furthermore, since we are the only true Christians, anyone outside of our group is among the deceived.)
- 2 Cor 10:5: "We demolish arguments and every pretension that sets itself up against the knowledge of God." (Opposing our theology is the same as opposing God.)
- 2 Cor 11:6: "I may indeed be untrained as a speaker, but I do have knowledge." (Regardless of our individual educational or theological backgrounds, even if we are biblical and literal illiterates, God has gifted every gnostic with the truth.)

There are many more such "knowledge" references throughout Paul's writings, and Valentinus shared his teachings with his audience in a manner that made it seem as though he was merely conveying the theology found in the writings of the apostle Paul. But that was merely the first act of his well-conceived performance. Valentinus possessed a remarkable insight into the human psyche and was truly a masterful showman. Once he had their attention, he convinced his potential converts that they were uniquely exceptional people—the elite.

He told his followers that they were "called" and "glorified" and personally given "the gift of knowing [the Father] by the power of the Logos." He followed that up by telling them that they were the very ones "whose name the Father has pronounced" and that "the Father knows the things that are yours, so that you may rest yourselves in them."[4]

You will notice the obvious flaw in Valentinus's interpretation of these verses as a personal message directed at his followers. Even if legitimate Scripture says or implies some of those things, it does not state anywhere that any specific gnostic can "know" for sure that he is "from above."[5] When you look beyond the appealing surface and strive to uncover the truth, you will recognize that Valentinus and all who use this line of reasoning are essentially saying that if you are a member of my church, believe exactly as I do, and adhere to the standards outlined in our charter, then yes, you can apply the verse to yourself and be absolutely sure that you are saved. Valentinus masterfully employed circular reasoning, clearly understanding that it was the sole method by which individuals could achieve their own sense of certainty regarding salvation and spiritual assurance.

In 1993, Kenneth Gentry wrote, "[Absolute assurance] requires a revelation beyond the Scriptures, because the Bible does not speak specifically to the individual in question. Nowhere in the Bible do we learn that Ken Gentry is among the elect."[6]

When we consider Gentry's assertions in the context of the gnostics, one might argue that there is no assurance that Joe the gnostic is certainly a heaven-bound Christian currently living on earth. The scriptural author may have been encouraging humble Christians who were facing unbearable persecution, such as crucifixion or being fed to the lions, to follow through till the end in faith. They had reached the point where they found themselves on the hill or in the arena because they were devoted enough to be willing to "give their lives for Christ's sake." Anyone would be terrified in the moments preceding such a gruesome and painful death, and clinging to those words might keep them from being one of those who, at the last minute, "shrink back and are destroyed" (Heb 10:39). It was widely accepted

---

4. Barnstone, *Other Bible*, 291, 294, 297.
5. Barnstone, *Other Bible*, 292.
6. Gentry, "Assurance and Lordship Salvation," 2.

in the early centuries that martyrdom was the only near-certain guarantee of salvation. Valentinus, on the other hand, convinced his audience that the promise of salvation was extended to every gnostic, including even the more casual and hedonistic Christians among them. He argued that simply by attending his church and embracing his teachings, they were assured a place in God's eternity.

This is not to say that some of his followers did not repent and give up the everyday pleasure-loving lives they would have lived as Roman citizens. Some gnostics reportedly led pure lives, while others, believing that the body was of no importance, took a different approach by indulging in sexual excess and materialism. But, regardless of their level of commitment, their faith was in Valentinus and not in Christ.

Even martyrdom was only a near-certain salvific guarantee, as there were many heretical groups in the early centuries, and some members of those groups died at the hands of the Romans. Regardless of what a person actually believed, simply being labeled a Christian was enough to endanger your life and your health. But heretical martyrdom ultimately does not pave the way to salvation. One of the writings of the man who was bishop of Carthage, Saint Cyprian (c. AD 200–258), might be helpful in giving us some grasp of the theological realities of the early Christian era.[7] He denied the appellation *martyr* for those who were murdered by the Romans for calling themselves Christians, when in actuality they were engaged in the worship of something or someone other than Christ. Cyprian realized that the Romans weren't exactly splitting hairs and carefully differentiating between factions and were therefore murdering supposed Christians from various heretical groups. In light of this, he wrote that one "cannot be a martyr who is not in the Church."[8] In other words, Cyprian was soberly stating that some of those being crucified, fed to the lions, tortured to death, and otherwise brutalized were outside of Christianity and therefore not to be classified as Christian martyrs. They may have been sincere and supremely committed to their beliefs, but, according to Cyprian, the beliefs they were dying for were not Christian.

How individual gnostics chose to live is not the issue; the critical point is that they were dedicating their present and future lives entirely to Valentinus while believing they were devoting themselves to God. Even more significantly, they believed they were not in need of any genuine spiritual

---

7. Carranza, *Battle for the Divinity*, 29.
8. Boer, *St. Ignatius of Antioch*, 28.

growth or a deeper understanding of Scripture beyond what they already possessed. They believed that they had already reached their spiritual destination and were assured of their salvation as long as they deepened their descent into Gnosticism. What they interpreted as spiritual growth was actually a greater commitment to Valentinus and his teachings, which was merely intensifying their fanaticism for an erroneous belief system. This course is often the most tragic result of Gnosticism, as it stifles the desire for actual spiritual growth and genuine faith in Christ. As I often heard the late Chuck Missler say, "The only certain barrier to truth is the perception that you already have it."

Their faulty conclusions regarding their salvation arose solely from a mutual dance between Valentinus's manipulation and the listener's ego. However, posing just a couple of straightforward questions could effectively undermine the entire argument, both in the past and in the present. For example, one might ask, "Valentinus, are you really claiming that anyone who reads these verses and adheres to your interpretation can be absolutely certain of their salvation?" It's evident that everyone looking from the outside at those employing this line of reasoning recognizes the absurdity of such a claim.

This is always the case when individuals self-righteously use Bible verses to point to themselves. The same pattern would become ubiquitous after the sixteenth century as a form of religious competition emerged, where leaders sought to make the concept of salvation more accessible to the masses, employing various strategies and doctrines to garner converts. Or, as will be discussed later, consider Dietrich Bonhoeffer's concept of "cheap grace": "The outcome of the Reformation was the victory, not of Luther's perception of grace in all its purity and costliness, but of the vigilant religious instinct of man for the place where grace is to be obtained at the cheapest price. All that was needed was a subtle and almost imperceptible change of emphasis, and the damage was done."[9]

We know how to ask ourselves the right questions when we want to. Most of us, after hearing the invitation of the well-dressed young Mormon boy who knocks on our door, don't rush down and sign up to become "gods of our own little planet." We also refrain from sending five thousand dollars to the obviously sketchy TV evangelist who cleverly twists legitimate scriptural passages to convince us of our salvation as long as we show our faith by quickly calling with our credit card number.

---

9. Bonhoeffer, *Cost of Discipleship*, 49.

FAKE SALVATION IN MODERN GNOSTIC AMERICA

Likewise, the gnostic followers should have been able to see through this enticement. The "Christ" of Valentinus, in concert with his theology, became incarnate to bring gnosis ("secret knowledge") to the earth. Because of the lack of "strict boundaries" in their writings, there were also other gnostic views of Christ that were developed by offshoot groups later on. After the discovery of the Nag Hammadi library, historians discovered the truth of the adage "Be careful what you wish for," as the 1945 discovery led to more questions than answers and more disagreement and controversy than historical agreement. However, in spite of the ongoing debates and the plethora of contradictory information, their basic gnostic system did come into sharper focus with the discovery of the gnostics' own words.

The gnostics believed that they themselves were the only ones who had the secret knowledge and the truth about God. Therefore, they considered all other groups ignorant because these others lacked the secret knowledge and the truth about God. It's patently clear that truth is in the eye of the beholder, as is falsehood. Of course, the same is true today, as no group sees itself as heretical. If any group did consider its theology heretical, it could easily remedy the situation by embracing a more accurate theology than the one currently held, which is something that religious groups rarely do. This is why the clarifications and conditions in the New Testament writings are rarely applied honestly and effectively. Every group views the statements that apply to true believers and heaven as relevant to their group and, conversely, all the statements that apply to being misled and deceived as relevant to other groups. That's followed by circular logic in which groups claim that they themselves are the true believers while others are merely professing believers; therefore, all of the positive biblical words are meant for them and their theological compatriots. As was true back then and is equally true today, group pride renders the New Testament conditions and safeguards difficult, if not impossible, to be used as intended.

Gnostics proclaimed that the culmination of secret knowledge reached its pinnacle when you came to know who you really were (a preordained, heaven-bound spirit trapped in a human body) and when you yourself affirmed the invisible, incomprehensible, absolute knowledge of your real self. The Valentinian gnostics capitalized on the fact that this cleverly crafted theology was very difficult to counter because genuine Scripture "proved" the validity of the converts' own self-assessment. Every time Paul used the word *know* or *knowledge*, it was not only an exclusive reference to all gnostics but also an unassailable affirmation of every gnostic's eternal place with the Father. Thus, as a gnostic, you could "know" with certainty that you were one of the chosen of God, being indwelled with his divine spark, and certain to be one of those who ascends to heaven.

The above paragraph may sound strikingly familiar because of its unmistakable parallel with many of today's modern Christian messages. These modern messages are designed, as were the gnostic messages, in the interest of popular appeal and church growth. More eerily, wording and utilization that are similar to those of the gnostics are still used today—or, more to the point, misused in order to pander to human pride, exclusivity, elitism, the authority of one's own spiritual self-assessment, and the handing out of eternal guarantees, with scriptural-sounding justifications.

Just as some do today, Valentinus fed his audience a string of rhetorical questions that virtually no one, in their own self-assessment, could answer in the negative. Valentinus lifted portions from the Gospels that appeared to support his theology and pieced them together in the gnostic Bible, which he arrogantly called the "Gospel of Truth." In the following excerpts from the Gospel of Truth, he asks if they personally believe that they love and know the truth, are joined with the Holy Spirit, know the Father and the Son, are in the light, and whether they consider themselves God's children.

The Gospel of Truth says,

> For each one loves truth because truth is the mouth of the Father. His tongue is the Holy Spirit, who joins him to truth.[10]
>
> He gave them the means of knowing the knowledge of the Father and the revelation of his son. . . . Say then in your heart that you are this perfect day and that in you the light which does not fail dwells.[11]
>
> Do not be a place of the devil, for you have already destroyed him.[12]
>
> Such are they who possess from above something of this immeasurable greatness, as they strain towards that unique and perfect one who exists there for them. And they do not go down to Hades. They have neither envy nor moaning, nor is death in them. But they rest in him who rests, without wearying themselves or becoming involved in the search for truth. But, they, indeed, are the

10. Barnstone, *Other Bible*, 293.
11. Barnstone, *Other Bible*, 294.
12. Barnstone, *Other Bible*, 294.

> truth, and the Father is in them, and they are in the Father, since they are perfect, inseparable from him who is truly good. They lack nothing in any way, but they are given rest and are refreshed by the Spirit. And they listen to their root; they have leisure for themselves, they in whom he will find his root, and he will suffer no loss to his soul.[13]
>
> The Father is good. And his children are perfect and worthy of his name, because he is the Father. Children of this kind are those whom he loves.[14]

Valentinus used his own Gospel of Truth, and not unedited genuine Scripture, because his message and guarantees would have been challenged by the qualifications and admonishments that are prevalent throughout the New Testament. As the late John Gerstner writes, "All Paul's letters are to professing Christians, some of whom are genuine and some of whom are not. In 2 Corinthians 13:5 he asks these professing Christians to examine themselves to see which they are, and he regularly does the same in his other letters. . . . Paul never assumes that all his readers were converted persons."[15] All of the New Testament is written to professing Christians; as such, Valentinus or any preacher could not legitimately use the verses where one is said to know something and apply it to everyone listening or everyone who simply reads that verse.

So, it's now obvious why the gnostic message spread like wildfire and not only was highly successful and popular but also posed a formidable, almost backbreaking challenge to the proto-orthodox. In the following chapter, we will examine Philip Lee's claims about the presence of Gnosticism within the modern American church.

---

13. Barnstone, *Other Bible*, 297.
14. Barnstone, *Other Bible*, 297.
15. Gerstner, *Wrongly Dividing the Word*, 439.

CHAPTER 2

GNOSTIC AMERICA

THE GREAT NINETEENTH-CENTURY CHURCH historian Philip Schaff stated that "American Christianity [is] a Motley sampling of all church history. All the powers of Europe, good and bad, are fermenting together under new and peculiar conditions."[1] When Philip Schaff died in 1893, the decay of the American church was nowhere near its nadir. In fact, it may only have been at the halfway point because in the past two hundred years, "a form of Christianity quite different from any known on the [European] Continent or in the British Isles [has] become the typical religion of North America."[2] This "different form of Christianity" advanced incrementally until shortly after World War II. Then the bottom fell out, and American Christianity has been in accelerated free fall ever since.

In his book *The Religious Crisis of the 1960s*, Hugh McLeod states, "The 1960s [saw] a rupture as profound as that brought about by the Reformation. The seventeenth, eighteenth, and nineteenth centuries had seen the gradual introduction of religious toleration and a trend toward greater religious pluralism." He noted that by "the 1970s, Western societies were pluralist, post-Christian, or secular." It was "a culmination of a long-term process of secularization, going back to the Renaissance and the Reformation; a progressive marginalization of [the Christian] religion."[3]

In addition to an increase in general "hedonism, there was [the society-altering influence of] the sexual revolution. [However], most important

1. Lee, *Against the Protestant Gnostics*, 84.
2. Lee, *Against the Protestant Gnostics*, 83.
3. McLeod, *Religious Crisis*, 1, 2, 8.

was the impact of affluence.... Most Western countries were in the middle of a period of unparalleled prosperity."[4] "There had been a progressive marginalization of religion and a more acute phase of this long-term crisis, arising from inexorable processes of modernization and rationalization, as more and more areas of life became subject to human knowledge and control."[5]

In the previous paragraph, McLeod describes a form of Christianity that increasingly approaches the domain of sensual, material secularism, where a more significant portion of life becomes "subject to human knowledge and control." While that description touches upon some of the key elements of contemporary Gnosticism, there exists a pivotal book that delves deeply into the intricacies of the entire subject. In 1987, Philip Lee released his detailed and enlightening book titled *Against the Protestant Gnostics*. This exceptional book provides a thorough and comprehensive exploration of Gnosticism, shedding light on its underlying principles and offering critical insights into its relationship with American Protestantism. Lee's meticulous examination is essential for anyone seeking to understand the complexities of modern Gnosticism.

In the introduction, Lee stated his purpose clearly: "This work attempts to demonstrate that Gnosticism is as close at hand as the reality we call Protestantism."[6] With this compelling assertion as his foundation, he devotes the next 347 pages to meticulously building his argument, weaving together historical contexts, theological nuances, and persuasive evidence to reinforce his premise.

Lee starts by identifying the origins of a dangerous trap that many American Protestant churches have unknowingly entered. McLeod echoes Lee's perspective, tracing the origins of contemporary challenges back to the pivotal Reformation period. Furthermore, as I will delve into later, McLeod extends this historical exploration even further, linking it to the influential era of the Renaissance. Various aspects of the Reformation play into eventual outcomes, regardless of whether the focus of a particular author is the rise of secularism, the encroachment of humanism, or the allure of Gnosticism. Each of these movements has, in its own way, contributed to the erosion of Christian values and teachings, painting a complex picture of the challenges faced by Protestantism.

4. McLeod, *Religious Crisis*, 14–15, 102.
5. McLeod, *Religious Crisis*, 8–9.
6. Lee, *Against the Protestant Gnostics*, xiv.

The early reformers recognized that they were setting up shop very close to the borders of Gnosticism. As Lee writes, "For Luther, Calvin, and also for Zwingli, there was a renewed preoccupation with the saving knowledge of God. [These] strong gnostic themes would be taken out of context by later Protestantism and carried to *dangerous* extremes."[7]

All three of the abovementioned reformers were highly knowledgeable theologians. Like experts in any field, they could approach theological peril closely without entering dangerous territory, just as professionals who work on high-voltage electric lines can venture where novices should not go. While all three knew that some of their theology was dangerously close to Gnosticism, they were skilled enough to stop before they reached the precipice. Lee points out that many of their followers did not have the skill to avoid "out of context" and "dangerous extremes."

In his book *The Cost of Discipleship*, Dietrich Bonhoeffer clearly reinforces the same point as Lee when stating, "Luther had said that grace alone can save; his followers took up his doctrine and repeated it word for word. But they left out the [answer]. His followers changed the answer into data for a calculation of their own.... Grace as the data for our calculations means grace at the cheapest price, but grace as the answer to the sum means costly grace. It is terrifying to realize what can be made of a genuine evangelical doctrine. In both cases, we have the identical formula—justification by faith alone. Yet the misuse of this formula leads to a complete destruction of its very essence."[8]

As mentioned in the last chapter, "The Gnostic texts were written so that the Gnostics could know [the certainty of] their own salvation."[9] Valentinus found that genuine Scripture, even with his imposed interpretations, would only get him so far in his aims. He, therefore, had to fabricate his own "sacred scriptures" that stated exactly what he wanted them to say. This was only possible in the early centuries before the New Testament had been codified and circulated. Indeed, from the sixteenth century on, no one except Joseph Smith was going to be able to get away with elevating their own fabricated books to the level of authoritative Scripture. Therefore, later Protestant leaders descending into Gnosticism or cheap grace had to hijack enlightened Protestant doctrine and then "take it out of context" or "misuse" it.

---

7. Lee, *Against the Protestant Gnostics*, 55; emphasis added.
8. Bonhoeffer, *Cost of Discipleship*, 49–50, 51.
9. Lee, *Against the Protestant Gnostics*, 4.

FAKE SALVATION IN MODERN GNOSTIC AMERICA

Lee argues that the concept of justification by faith alone has been "taken out of context," while Bonhoeffer contends that this formulation has been "misused." In both instances, it was employed in a way similar to how Valentinus utilized his fraudulent Bible texts, allowing modern gnostic Protestants to feel assured of their own salvation. Both express this sentiment in their own ways. Religious elitism, self-concentration, self-conceit, and self-exultation are ubiquitous throughout Lee's book. He speaks of "Protestant narcissism"[10] and the monotonous religious hymn echoing from the 1970s till today where the "beat goes, me, me, me, me . . ."[11] Bonhoeffer is more succinct in declaring that he "considered self-righteousness and complacency great sins against the Holy Spirit."[12]

Philip Lee and Dietrich Bonhoeffer have much in common, even though Bonhoeffer was executed by the Nazis back in 1945. Lee calls modern American Christianity "Post-Christian" by demonstrating that its deception is rooted in Gnosticism, while Bonhoeffer posthumously arrives at the same conclusion by demonstrating that its deception is rooted in cheap grace. Even eighty years after his death, his writings reprove modern American Protestantism and leave no doubt that the pervasive concept of "cheap grace" permeates contemporary sermons, the modern church growth movement, and all the American guarantees of salvation. As Bonhoeffer says, "Cheap grace is the grace we bestow on ourselves."[13] It's "a secularized Christianity"; it's "man seeking his own interests."[14]

I've included a few insightful quotes from Bonhoeffer. Following that will be quotes from Lee, most of which, in some way, will highlight the two men's shared perspectives.

Bonhoeffer states, "Cheap grace is the deadly enemy of our church"; "Cheap grace means grace sold on the market"; "Cheap grace means grace as a doctrine, a principle, a system."[15]

> It is under the influence of this kind of grace that the world has been made Christian, but at the cost of secularizing the Christian religion as never before. The upshot of it all is that my only duty as a Christian is to leave the world for an hour or so on a

---

10. Lee, *Against the Protestant Gnostics*, 197.
11. Lee, *Against the Protestant Gnostics*, 198.
12. Bonhoeffer, *Cost of Discipleship*, 24.
13. Bonhoeffer, *Cost of Discipleship*, 44.
14. Bonhoeffer, *Cost of Discipleship*, 49.
15. Bonhoeffer, *Cost of Discipleship*, 43.

Sunday morning and go to church to be assured that my sins are all forgiven.[16]

We were told that our salvation had already been accomplished. Deceived and weakened, men felt that they were strong now that they were in possession of this cheap grace.[17]

Luther's formula has been repeated, but its truth perverted into self-deception. Cheap grace had won the day.[18]

Bonhoeffer's quotes are straightforward and self-explanatory. In contrast, Lee's quotes, much like his intricate book, are so densely packed with insight and complexity that they can be challenging to comprehend when considered on their own. To address this complexity, I will incorporate Lee's quotes as I weave them into a broader narrative context. This approach will not only enhance clarity but will also make the connections more relatable and accessible when I refer to any of them later in the book.

"The decline of authentic Protestantism and the ascendancy of gnostic Christianity in North America has wrought horrendous results."[19] Why? As mentioned earlier, "the great reformers [were] very close to adopting a form of Christian Gnosticism"[20] but were good enough theologians to avoid crossing that dangerous frontier. While Luther, Zwingli, and Calvin were acutely aware of the treacherous terrain they were carefully navigating, later Protestants seemed oblivious to the minefield and swiftly rushed through in their eagerness to establish their own denominations.

These later Protestants should have noticed that others had laid out signs warning of the "ominous connection between medieval gnosis and the Reformation,"[21] highlighting the danger posed by the fact that "the mighty acts of God are being replaced by a knowledge that saves."[22] Moreover, various smaller signs warned that "the Puritan changes in New England theology [come] perilously close to Gnostic Christianity. Of particular concern is the Puritans' concentration on self and their tendency to regard humanity from an elitist perspective."[23]

16. Bonhoeffer, *Cost of Discipleship*, 50–51.
17. Bonhoeffer, *Cost of Discipleship*, 55.
18. Bonhoeffer, *Cost of Discipleship*, 53.
19. Lee, *Against the Protestant Gnostics*, 189.
20. Lee, *Against the Protestant Gnostics*, 54.
21. Lee, *Against the Protestant Gnostics*, 55.
22. Lee, *Against the Protestant Gnostics*, 55.
23. Lee, *Against the Protestant Gnostics*, 74.

Then, a massive billboard alerting them to a significant historical reality: "The Calvinism of the 16th century took root in regions which had been Cathar strongholds in the 13th [century]."[24] It's common knowledge that the theology of the Cathars was rooted in Gnosticism. They upheld a classic form of gnostic dualism, viewing the God of the Old Testament as evil and contrasting him with the God of the New Testament, who was good.

And finally, a sign admonishing them to slow down and ask themselves if modern American "Protestantism was another instance of Gnostic tendency finally taking root on inviting soil."[25]

But why be watchful of Gnosticism? Why not just ignore "the close connection between the revolutionary spirit of the 18th century and evangelical Protestantism"?[26] After all, during that time, everyone was anxious to discard our "British heritage [and the] historic church."[27] Furthermore, the people who would later join American churches already believed the "elitist notion that Americans are God's chosen people."[28] Conveniently, their leaders could build their talking points around the fact that "American Protestantism feels that the United States is a chosen nation."[29] They could all continue down the gnostic path by overlooking the New Testament's emphasis on humility while simultaneously failing to note that "Gnosticism is always an elitist faith."[30]

What was needed was a new kind of church for self-centered twentieth-century people. "Within this new type of church, saving knowledge would become the one test of authenticity."[31] They also found the Great Apostasy theory useful, as it suggested that the true church had been lost in the early centuries of Christianity, leading to a significant departure from its original apostolic teachings. This perspective allowed them to reject the theological frameworks established by the Catholic and Greek Orthodox Churches, as well as the decisions made during the various church councils, all of which took place after the reign of Constantine. Furthermore, they could set aside

---

24. Lee, *Against the Protestant Gnostics*, 55.
25. Lee, *Against the Protestant Gnostics*, 55.
26. Lee, *Against the Protestant Gnostics*, 88.
27. Lee, *Against the Protestant Gnostics*, 88.
28. Lee, *Against the Protestant Gnostics*, 168, 169.
29. Lee, *Against the Protestant Gnostics*, 169.
30. Lee, *Against the Protestant Gnostics*, 11.
31. Lee, *Against the Protestant Gnostics*, 57.

the contributions of key Protestant reformers such as Martin Luther, Ulrich Zwingli, and John Calvin. Their disagreements with one another highlight a fundamental division, suggesting that they retained too many elements of Catholic doctrine and the councils they sought to reform. Additionally, the Radical Reformers rejected the ideas of the Magisterial Reformation shortly after the Reformation began, leaving them behind by the middle of the sixteenth century.

The strategy for success was this: "The Norman Vincent Peale theology has culminated in the Church Growth movement. The philosophy behind this movement is that if local churches want to grow, they must find out what the people want and then give it to them."[32] This brings to mind a clever quip attributed to Adlai Stevenson: "I find St. Paul appealing, and St. Peale appalling."

But they had to avoid certain things: "What kind of organization would have the nerve to call modern men and women into a life of self-denial rather than a life of self-acceptance, [especially] in an age of self-seeking instant gratification?"[33] That would be "assisted religious suicide."[34] But this wouldn't: "The central, unique feature of American Christianity [is] that individuals not only do choose Jesus, but choose him on their own terms."[35] These emotional, self-righteous men and women are already convinced "of the reliability of the individual heart,"[36] so a good place to start might be "the emphasis on salvation in terms of the individual experience of the believer"[37]—perhaps even expressly encouraging emotionalism and reinforcing the individual's belief that their inner feelings are trustworthy spiritual messages.

Gnosticism relies heavily on the inner emotions of its members. Akin to the Mormon "burning in the bosom," every personally edifying emotion is perceived as being spiritually generated rather than self-generated. It would be beneficial to present the reliability of personal emotionalism in a well-organized procedure, or as Lee says, "The salvation of Christ became a formula in North America . . . [based on the] emotion of the individual

---

32. Lee, *Against the Protestant Gnostics*, 210.
33. Lee, *Against the Protestant Gnostics*, 256.
34. Which is also the title of chapter 6 in Eberstadt, *How the West Really Lost*.
35. Lee, *Against the Protestant Gnostics*, 156.
36. Lee, *Against the Protestant Gnostics*, 148.
37. Lee, *Against the Protestant Gnostics*, 104.

soul."[38] "Observe the American fascination with technique. For evangelicals, conversion is a technique, a necessary one, for salvation."[39]

They just had to make sure that their members dismissed reality and did not see themselves in any way when looking at the cults since "Gnostic cults are but caricatures of the more subtle Gnosticism within the Protestant Church itself."[40]

An exploration of the similarities between contemporary Protestantism and American cults will be undertaken in a forthcoming chapter because Protestantism's "present entanglements with Gnosticism cannot be escaped until Protestant church people are prepared to be honestly critical of their own religion, and then determine to do something about it."[41]

38. Lee, *Against the Protestant Gnostics*, 102.
39. Lee, *Against the Protestant Gnostics*, 109.
40. Lee, *Against the Protestant Gnostics*, 159.
41. Lee, *Against the Protestant Gnostics*, 218.

CHAPTER 3

LORD, LORD

IN THE PREVIOUS CHAPTER, Philip Lee explained why virtually every one of the reported thirty-five thousand modern Protestant churches is awarding guaranteed salvation to their followers. The simple reason is that American Protestantism has become deeply entrenched in Gnosticism, fitting the textbook definition perfectly. The assurance of salvation is the central tenet within the gnostic framework, emphasizing the idea that individuals can attain a profound sense of security regarding their eternal destiny.

Throughout Christian history, Gnosticism has consistently focused on the goal of ensuring salvation for its followers, often resorting to extreme measures to achieve this aim. Many modern preachers have made this guarantee so simple that one can join a radio or TV preacher in the sinner's prayer and then be told that they are now saved and cannot lose their salvation. The same promises are routinely made at church services and large crusades at baseball stadiums. Pastor Kyle Idleman, in his book *Not a Fan*, makes this interesting observation:

> Many of our churches in America have gone from being sanctuaries to becoming stadiums. And every week, all the fans come to the stadium where they cheer for Jesus.[1]

Then, after remorsefully confessing that he had been one of those who preached a watered-down gospel for personal profit, he said this:

> Do you remember reading the story in the news about the conviction of a pharmacist named Robert Courtney? He was convicted

1. Idleman, *Not a Fan*, 25.

of diluting the medication of cancer patients in order to make a profit. Over a period of about nine years, he diluted an estimated 98,000 prescriptions of medications affecting some 42,000 patients. At least 17 cancer patients died after receiving diluted formulation of chemotherapy. He made some 19 million dollars from the fraud. Robert was sentenced to 30 years in prison. A man had been entrusted with the responsibility of handing out life-saving medication; but for the sake of personal gain diluted it to the point where it couldn't help people. That's a picture of what many preachers, including myself, are guilty of doing.[2]

Obviously, all these assurances from radio and television, along with the guarantees of salvation offered through altar calls, cannot be legitimate. We are very astute in recognizing that "the church across the street" has no right to give away salvation. Moreover, all of Protestantism universally recognizes that exclusivist groups like the Jehovah's Witnesses and the Mormons have no right to guarantee their members' salvation, let alone claim that their church is the only saving church.

Could it be that the Jehovah's Witnesses, Mormons, and every church that offers guaranteed salvation hold an equal standing in terms of their validity or lack thereof? In other words, is it possible that each and every one of them lacks legitimacy in that regard?

In Matt 7, Jesus addresses this critical topic concerning the authenticity of faith. He emphasizes that there are many people who firmly believe they will enter the kingdom of heaven but will ultimately be rejected on the last day.

"Not every one that saith unto me, Lord, Lord, shall enter into the kingdom of heaven; but he that doeth the will of my Father which is in heaven. Many will say to me in that day, Lord, Lord, have we not prophesied in thy name? and in thy name have cast out devils? and in thy name done many wonderful works? And then will I profess unto them, I never knew you: depart from me, ye that work iniquity" (Matt 7:21–23).

Even a cursory look at these verses can spark some intriguing thoughts. In the first verse, Christ informs us that people will approach him on the last day convinced of their salvation because they have met their own standard of what it means to do God's will. We all know atheists who claim to meet this standard, especially those who are fanatically involved in charitable endeavors. Of course, Christians know that "the work of God

---

2. Idleman, *Not a Fan*, 165–66.

is to believe in the one that he sent" (John 6:29), but the point here is that even some atheists believe in their hearts that they meet the superficial understanding of this standard. They don't realize that their own heart is not a reliable witness since "the heart is deceitful above all things" (Jer 17:9).

In the next sentence, Christ tells us that many are self-deluded. It's not a small minority that falsely believes that they have met the standard of faith; it's apparently the majority. And from a human perspective, they seem to have had good reason to believe that their faith is real. They apparently have enough faith to legitimately cast out devils and do miracles.

But the most enlightening part of that entire section of Scripture is that Christ himself is apparently saying that no one will know the certainty of their salvation until the very last day.

Obviously, that's just my own brief opinion about that section of Scripture. However, in the prior chapter, we explored the profound insights of an actual, highly qualified theologian. Dietrich Bonhoeffer wrote about the misinterpretations of Martin Luther's writings and argued that these distortions led to the emergence of a pervasive church model characterized by what he called "cheap grace." Bonhoeffer critically examined the contemporary interpretation of grace, which he argues is often shallow and lacking depth. This superficial understanding leads to a weakened conception of genuine spirituality within the church, diminishing Luther's original perception of grace. Bonhoeffer stresses that such a diluted perspective fails to engage the profound and radical implications of grace that are essential for authentic Christian faith and practice.

Bonhoeffer offers a qualified and powerful commentary on Matt 7:21–23. He writes: "The man who says 'Lord, Lord' has either called himself to Jesus without the Holy Spirit or else has made out the call of Jesus as a personal privilege. Here is the most serious, most incredible satanic possibility in the church: the final division, which only occurs on the last day. Jesus [says] to the last of the rejected: I have never known you."[3]

Bonhoeffer agrees with Jesus and says that we will only know if we are saved on the last day. Only on that day will we find out if we had demonic faith, false faith, or no faith. Lutheranism has always had an issue with the perseverance of one's faith, and even Calvinism, which solved the perseverance to their own satisfaction, had an issue with differentiating between genuine faith and false faith. Calvinists could only differentiate with certainty when looking backward. The man who was a member of the

---

3. Bonhoeffer, *Cost of Discipleship*, 195.

Calvinist church and then rejected it could be seen in the rearview mirror as one who never had genuine faith in the first place. The uncertainties of both Calvinism and Lutheranism are outlined by noted theologian Professor Phillip Cary. He states,

> [Are] you saved? Luther [says] you have to not only be justified now by faith in Christ, you have to be justified on the day of your death. You'll have to know that you're going to persevere. How can you possibly know that? Augustine [agrees]: You can't know if you're going to persevere in faith to the end. How could you? That's the future.[4]

> Calvin disagrees with Augustine [even though he took his entire predestination concept from Augustine]. Calvin proposes this radical innovation: He says you can know that you're predestined to be saved. [Which means you've had the] inner call [commonly known in Protestantism as a true conversion experience]. The Holy Spirit changes your heart [and] converts your heart so that now you have true . . . and saving faith. After this point, you have a faith that is guaranteed to last.[5]

Luther argues that it's impossible to be sure of one's perseverance in faith, while Calvin maintains that such assurance is indeed possible. Calvin's ideas on predestination are rooted in the writings of Augustine, who never denied the existence of free will. Although Augustine wavered on the concept of predestination, he never went anywhere near Calvin's innovation of double predestination, where he says that some individuals are predestined for salvation while others are predestined for hell. That notion contradicts the fundamental invitations found throughout the entire Bible, as well as the choices we are continually called to make. We constantly choose between fleeting moments of time and everlasting life, good and evil, Satan and God, while simultaneously grappling with the tension between self-serving desires and the selflessness exemplified by Christ.

> The inner call gives you this new kind of faith, another innovation [of] Calvin. There is such a thing as a temporary false faith [however, and you will need] to be able to recognize the difference. [How?] If you've had this inner call, this effectual call of the Holy Spirit converting your will, then you know [you're saved]. There

---

4. Cary, *History of Christian Theology*, 305 (transcript from lecture 20, "Calvin and Reformed Theology").

5. Cary, *History of Christian Theology*, 305–6, 307.

are people who have a kind of pseudo-conversion who think they have saving faith, but [they don't].⁶

For Calvin, true faith [unlike temporary false faith] can't be lost. [However] anytime someone abandons Christianity, that shows that they never really had true faith. . . . [The presence or absence of a more religious lifestyle and/or] the fruits of the Spirit [can provide meaningful insights, but not a definitive answer on true or false faith]. How [then] do you know which kind of faith you have [for only true faith leads to] assurance of salvation? [This issue is] crucial for Calvinist pastoral care.⁷

Many have noted that the "inner call" described by Calvin is quite similar to the Mormon concept of the "burning in the bosom." Throughout Christian history, this personal emotional response has always come from within the individual's mind and gut, making it ultimately unreliable.

Differentiating between authentic and inauthentic faith often involves a self-serving approach, where individuals within religious contexts rely on circular reasoning to reach conclusions that provide them with a sense of validation. This introspective process enables them to arrive at predetermined notions of "proof" regarding their beliefs. With the use of Andreas Bergman's extraordinary thesis, I will delve deeper into this use of circular reasoning very shortly. Bergman also emphasizes that a significant aspect of pastoral care involves providing spiritual and emotional support, which is akin to therapy. This approach is centered on reassuring individuals that, despite their lingering doubts and uncertainties, they are still embraced and valued members of the church community. The aim is to foster a sense of belonging and connection, helping them navigate their internal struggles while nurturing their faith.

When considering the positive transformations in one's lifestyle or the manifestation of the fruits of the Spirit that may have previously been absent, it becomes evident that even secular changes can demonstrate specific characteristics of these virtues. These transformations often reflect a newfound sense of purpose, compassion, and personal growth, highlighting the profound impact of such changes, whether they are inspired by spiritual beliefs or arise from secular influences.

For instance, an unhinged, violent methamphetamine addict would most certainly have positive changes that might appear religious after

---

6. Cary, *History of Christian Theology*, 307.
7. Cary, *History of Christian Theology*, 307, 308.

successful treatment at a secular drug intervention clinic. Following successful rehabilitation, he would likely demonstrate enhanced love, joy, peace, patience, kindness, goodness, and faithfulness (albeit in something other than meth), along with greater gentleness and much stronger self-control than he had previously shown. While all who knew him might marvel at the amazing transformation, only as a religious-themed joke would they say that he is now converted and "heaven-bound."

Bergman, too, makes a penetrating observation regarding the use of religious lifestyle changes and/or the fruits of the Spirit as a confirmation of genuine faith: "After all the arguments for the exclusion of works from justification [by the early reformers], works [are brought in] through the backdoor to condition the certitude of salvation."[8]

Cary continues with assurance:

> Luther didn't have Calvin's certainty or assurance of salvation. Lutheran anxiety is called Anfechtung [meaning] attack. [Lutherans must] just [keep] on hanging onto the promise of God and the Gospel.[9]
>
> The devil [is] saying, you're going to hell because you think you have faith [but you will not persevere]. Luther's theology doesn't have a way of arguing that you can be sure of your salvation. All you can do is hang onto the Gospel [every day of your life]. [Lutherans] have no hope whatsoever except [in] Jesus Christ.[10]

Echoing the fact that Luther didn't have Calvin's assurance of salvation, an article on "Luther's dark nights" states the following:

> A scant few years after the Reformation, in 1527 [Luther experienced one of his deepest depressions]....
>
> Historian David Steinmetz describes the terror which Luther [felt] as a fear that "God had turned his back on him once and for all," abandoning him "to suffer the pains of hell." Feeling "alone in the universe," Luther "doubted his own faith, his own mission, and the goodness of God—doubts which, because they verged on blasphemy, drove him deeper and deeper" into despair. His prayers met a "wall of indifferent silence." He experienced heart palpitations, crying spells, and profuse sweating. He was convinced that he would die soon and go straight to hell. "For more

---

8. Bergman, "Certainty of Salvation," 43.

9. Cary, *History of Christian Theology*, 309 (transcript from lecture 19, "Luther and Protestant Theology").

10. Cary, *History of Christian Theology*, 310.

than a week, I was close to the gates of death and hell. I trembled in all my members. Christ was wholly lost. I was shaken by desperation and blasphemy of God." His faith was as if it had never been. He "despised himself and murmured against God." Indeed, his friend Philip Melanchthon said that the terrors afflicting Luther became so severe that he almost died.[11]

Consider that this occurred a decade after Martin Luther boldly nailed his Ninety-Five Theses to the door of the Wittenberg church on October 31, 1517. To suggest that he sounded a little unsure about whether he was personally "justified by faith" would be an understatement.

Cary again says,

> If you need certainty and assurance of salvation, go with Calvinism [unless] you can't stand the thought of trying to figure out whether you have true faith [or the temporary, false kind of faith].[12]

> I couldn't possibly be a Calvinist. I can't possibly know that I have true faith. In any case, you're going to get anxiety one way or another.[13]

If you sense a sarcastic tone in Phillip Cary's remarks, you're absolutely on point. Earlier in his text, he suggests that no belief system offers an infallible path to guaranteed salvation. When he asserts, "If you need the certainty of assurance of salvation, go with Calvinism," it's clear he doesn't honestly believe that becoming a Calvinist ensures a spot in heaven; if he did, he would likely adopt that belief system himself.

When Cary writes, "You're going to experience anxiety one way or another," he clearly suggests that none of the systems truly offer genuine guarantees of salvation. He further implies that if you choose to deceive yourself, Calvinism stands out as the most appealing false promise among the available options. It's almost like saying, "If you decide to trust in the certainty of lucky omens, then placing a horseshoe over your door is a better option than merely waiting for a shooting star to appear."

Continuing along this line of thought, I now turn to the thesis by Andreas Bergman, aptly titled "The Certainty of Salvation in the Theology of Martin Chemnitz." Bergman presented his doctoral dissertation to the Faculty of Theology at the University of Helsinki on May 16, 2023.

---

11. "Martin Luther's Anfechtungen."
12. Cary, *History of Christian Theology*, 310.
13. Cary, *History of Christian Theology*, 310.

FAKE SALVATION IN MODERN GNOSTIC AMERICA

Martin Chemnitz, born in 1522, holds a significant place in the Evangelical Lutheran tradition, often referred to as the "Second Martin" in homage to the prominent Reformer Martin Luther. Renowned for his profound theological insights, Chemnitz emerged as a pivotal figure in Lutheranism, shaping its doctrines and practices during a transformative period in church history. His extensive writings and contributions have earned him recognition as one of the leading theologians and revered church fathers of the Lutheran faith, leaving a lasting impact on the development of Protestant theology.

His efforts were particularly instrumental in publishing the *Book of Concord*, a vital document that unified Lutheran teachings. The widely repeated saying, "If Martin Chemnitz had not come along, Martin Luther would hardly have survived," underscores the profound impact Chemnitz had during a crucial period in the Reformation. He could shed light on even the most intricate concepts, transforming confusion into clarity, which is why Bergman focused his dissertation on him rather than on Luther himself.

Bergman begins by using the term "The Protestant Dilemma," which he explains in the following words:

> Luther's thought assumes that if one wants to be infallibly certain of his salvation, they must be certain that their interpretation of the Bible is infallibly correct. Obviously, the concern that false exegesis threatens the certainty of salvation explains why Luther opposed Zwingli's doctrine of the Lord's Supper so strictly. And it should not surprise us that Luther felt that the Swiss had a different spirit than the Lutherans.[14]

> But there was a great dilemma. Various Protestant groups believed that they alone possessed the truth because they interpreted Scripture under the Holy Spirit's illumination, but they had little criteria to work with to distinguish between true and false certainty.[15]

While the above is brilliantly written and expressed, I'm sure many of you are wondering what it means in plain English. Basically, Luther believed he was saved because the same Spirit that revealed this truth to him also provided him with what he considered the "only correct" interpretation of Scripture and salvation. This perspective worked well for him, especially since it countered the centuries of beliefs and practices that had been added

---

14. Bergman, "Certainty of Salvation," 77.
15. Bergman, "Certainty of Salvation," 49.

to Scripture by the Catholic Church. In essence, it all worked as long as he remained the singular voice of the Reformation, the one individual through whom the Spirit was genuinely communicating.

However, shortly after Luther's break with Catholicism, Zwingli emerged with interpretations that deviated significantly from Luther's, particularly concerning the concept of Christ's real presence in the Lord's Supper. During their meeting in Marburg in 1529, it was reported that Luther was infuriated, allegedly pounding his fist on the table and shouting, "This is my body, this is my body . . ." Given the multitude of interpretations, denominations, and conflicting theologies that are prevalent today, it's hard for us to grasp the complex and pressing issues this raises. What's the big deal, and why couldn't Luther simply agree to disagree?

He absolutely could not agree to disagree. The stakes were exceptionally high, touching on critical theological principles, institutional integrity, and numerous vital implications that affected a wide range of areas. Most importantly, the real turmoil was brewing within Luther's own mind.

Great leaders like Luther exuded remarkable self-confidence, which was essential for taking a stand against the established order and challenging entrenched powerful authorities, such as the Catholic Church. He viewed Pope Leo X as "the antichrist" because the pope opposed Luther and sought to kill him. Luther sincerely believed that any intelligent individual reading Scripture under the guidance of the Spirit would interpret it in the same way he did. He regarded his interpretations as obviously true. Therefore, he concluded that the pope must possess a demonic spirit.

Luther understood that the pope was no fool; however, he believed that centuries of ingrained Catholic dogma had clouded his judgment, leaving him vulnerable to manipulation by Satan. Now, he's confronted by an obviously intelligent man, Zwingli, whose mind has not been clouded by Catholic dogma and is so blind that he can't even understand something as simple as "This is my body."

As mentioned earlier, the same spirit that assured Luther of his salvation also gave him a singular interpretation of Scripture. However, Zwingli's holding a different interpretation, also given to him by the Holy Spirit, raises the possibility of either multiple holy spirits, which is impossible, or it calls into question the validity of Luther's assumption of being saved. To preserve his certainty about his salvation, he assumes Zwingli "has a different spirit." This means that Zwingli, in some areas at least, must be under the same demonic influence as the pope.

Scripture alone relies on the perspicuity of Scripture, which means the Bible "is clear enough for anyone—even a child—to understand." That is the doctrine that the reformers endorsed as they "endeavored to return the church to the clearest, literal meaning of the Bible." Deuteronomy 6:6 "implies that the children are capable of understanding and applying the Word of God as their parents teach it to them. But note that it also implies that ordinary mothers and fathers are able to grasp Scripture sufficient enough to teach it to their children."[16]

Zwingli's differing view on Christ's real presence in the Lord's Supper raised significant concerns on several fronts. One major issue was that it posed a serious challenge to the foundational principle of Scripture alone. In Luther's mind, if something as clear and straightforward as "This is my body" is not meant to be taken as a literal statement that in some way means precisely what it says, then there's nothing in the Bible that means what it says; it's all allegorical. Luther argues that Zwingli's nonliteral interpretation raises questions about the fundamental nature of the Bible itself. In his eyes, if the most evident and straightforward words can be dismissed as figurative, then one must question the integrity of all scriptural text. This perspective threatens to undermine the validity of Scripture, rendering it entirely allegorical and ultimately devoid of real significance or authority.

And therein lies a graphic picture of the Protestant dilemma. Luther believes that he alone possesses the truth because he alone interpreted Scripture under the Holy Spirit's illumination. That same Spirit also gave him an inner feeling of security about his own salvation. Likewise, Zwingli believed that he alone possessed the truth because he alone interpreted Scripture under the illumination of the Holy Spirit. That same Spirit also gave him an inner feeling of security about his own salvation. But there was a great dilemma. Neither man had clear criteria to differentiate between true certainty and false certainty or to distinguish between true interpretation and false interpretation.

It's conceivable, given his remarkable intelligence, that Luther quickly imagined the future and predicted that, over the course of half a millennium, there could be an overwhelming proliferation of churches. He might have envisioned countless congregations emerging, each with their own distinct interpretations of sacred texts. If one individual chose to take a passage literally while another viewed it as allegorical, that difference in understanding could spark the creation of a new church. This cycle of

---

16. Ligonier Ministries, "Clarity of Scripture."

interpretation and divergence would likely continue indefinitely, leading to an ever-expanding tapestry of faiths and beliefs, which, in reality, has indeed come to pass.

From this point on, I will quote Bergman verbatim so that you can decipher what he's saying for yourself and confirm that my synopsis is accurate.

> In the skeptical context of the time, certitude was considered a sign of the work of the Holy Spirit, but there was a great dilemma. Various Protestant groups believed that they alone possessed the truth because they interpreted Scripture under the Holy Spirit's illumination, but they had little criteria to work with to distinguish between true and false certainty.[17]
>
> Along the way, we touched upon the theme that motivated our examination: the experience of certainty as the ultimate criterion of truth and the problem of circularity related to it. . . . We return to the Reformation era in search of answers to the great Protestant dilemma: various Protestant groups [claim] that they alone possess divine truth because they have the certainty that only the Holy Spirit may grant.[18]
>
> Furthermore, in Protestantism, the Holy Spirit also became the agent of exegetical certainty. All Protestants agreed that the fall had a negative effect on the noetic capabilities of human beings, and thus, only the Spirit could illumine the mind and provide a sure interpretation of Scripture. We previously noted that this belief resulted in a deep dilemma when the Protestant groups became divided over their interpretations of Scripture. Considering Luther's emphasis on the theology of the Word, we may understand that the dilemma posed an especially grave problem for him: Luther's thought assumes that if one wants to be infallibly certain of salvation, they must be certain that their interpretation of the Bible is infallibly correct. Obviously, the concern that false exegesis threatens the certainty of salvation explains why Luther opposed Zwingli's doctrine of the Lord's Supper so strictly. And it should not surprise us that Luther felt that the Swiss had a different spirit than the Lutherans.[19]
>
> Chemnitz goes on to answer Andrada's challenge that puts forward the dilemma of distinguishing the spirits.

---

17. Bergman, "Certainty of Salvation," 49.
18. Bergman, "Certainty of Salvation," 70.
19. Bergman, "Certainty of Salvation," 77.

Chemnitz's response is certainly not original. Just like Luther, he emphasizes the external Word as the criterion [for] discerning whether the source of our certainty is the Holy Spirit. He argues that because Scripture says that human beings receive the Holy Spirit through faith, they can be assured that the inner movements which follow from faith are from the Spirit. There are, however, two problems with this response. The first one is the certainty of having true faith: How can one be sure of possessing true faith in the biblical sense and, hence, the Holy Spirit? Chemnitz's criteria for true faith will be examined later, but they are undermined by the second problem, which is the certainty of one's interpretation of Scripture: How can Chemnitz be sure that his interpretation of the Bible's teaching on the sealing by the [Spirit] is correct? It probably comes as no surprise, however, that Chemnitz's answer to the "Protestant dilemma" is plagued by the same problem of circularity as Luther's.[20]

Although Chemnitz seeks to demonstrate that not only his doctrine but also his hermeneutics are based on Scripture, he fails to solve the "Protestant dilemma."[21]

CONCLUSIONS

Curiously, however, he still claims that believers can lose their salvation. He does not try to solve the apparent problem that emerges from the combination of the certainty of predestination and the possibility of lapsing from faith. How can one have an indubitable certainty of being predestined to eternal life if it is possible for them to lose their faith and end up in damnation?[22]

The indubitable certainty of salvation requires . . . that [your group's] interpretation of Scripture is trustworthy, despite other Protestants disagreeing on doctrinal positions and scriptural interpretation.[23]

---

20. Bergman, "Certainty of Salvation," 159.
21. Bergman, "Certainty of Salvation," 196.
22. Bergman, "Certainty of Salvation," 237.
23. Bergman, "Certainty of Salvation," 238.

Chemnitz's inclusion of the certainty of salvation in the essence of faith may cause some to be anxious about whether they have true faith if they have any doubts about their salvation.[24]

Chemnitz is willing to minimize the quality of faith, to undermine his scriptural definition of faith as assurance, for the sake of a pastoral need. With such a concession, he comes close to medieval pastoral theologians who also relied on minimization to prevent despair.... The purpose of the Word ... is to confer Christ's grace and provide certainty of salvation. According to Chemnitz, indubitable certainty of salvation presupposes that Christians can distinguish true faith from false faith.[25]

If a Christian cannot have indubitable certainty that their faith is genuine, they cannot have indubitable certainty of justification and predestination. This conditioning of the knowledge of salvation by one's works is one of the most significant weak points in Chemnitz's position on the indubitable certitude of salvation. After all the arguments for the exclusion of works from justification to guarantee the certainty of salvation, he brings works back through the backdoor to condition the certitude of salvation.[26]

If human knowledge of the canon is based on fallible human witnesses, one cannot be indubitably sure that they have the correct canon in their hands. This, evidently, undermines the reliability of the Bible as a trustworthy source of revelation.[27]

During the past few centuries, it has become less common for Lutherans to insist on the indubitability of the certainty of salvation.[28]

The indubitability of human assurance presumably reflects the post-17th century intellectual development on the unreliability or limited nature of human knowledge. As we noted earlier, in the 16th century, everyone was still convinced that human beings may have infallible religious certainty. In our current context, however, such optimism concerning human knowledge seems unwarranted for many.[29]

---

24. Bergman, "Certainty of Salvation," 238.
25. Bergman, "Certainty of Salvation," 239.
26. Bergman, "Certainty of Salvation," 241.
27. Bergman, "Certainty of Salvation," 242.
28. Bergman, "Certainty of Salvation," 243.
29. Bergman, "Certainty of Salvation," 244.

Chemnitz's teaching on the certainty of salvation does not warrant indubitable certainty.[30]

---

30. Bergman, "Certainty of Salvation," 244.

CHAPTER 4

PAINTED INTO A CORNER: DISPENSATIONALISM

DISPENSATIONALISM IS A THEOLOGICAL perspective that interprets history as a series of distinct periods, known as "dispensations," during which God interacts with humanity in varying ways. This belief system is currently the most widespread theological framework among evangelical Protestant communities in the United States. Many individuals may not fully recognize that their church adheres to this specific framework of belief. If your congregation teaches the concept of the rapture, it is quite probable that it is a dispensational church, regardless of its denominational affiliation or name on the door.

This theological perspective has significantly shaped American Christianity, influencing a wide range of sermons, teachings, and especially eschatological viewpoints across diverse congregations. The influence of this phenomenon manifests itself not only in the tenets of religious doctrine but also profoundly shapes how individuals experience and express their faith across a multitude of churches nationwide. This impact extends into the media landscape, significantly affecting Christianity's representation on radio and television. Furthermore, it plays a crucial role in the portrayal of Christian values, beliefs, and even vocabulary within both popular religious culture and broader society.

Dispensationalism emerged in the nineteenth century, primarily through the influential teachings of John Nelson Darby and the Plymouth Brethren. The time frame certainly aligns with the distorted nineteenth-century American religious mindset discussed in the introduction, and critics argue that some of that atmosphere has influenced its essence. In the twentieth century, this theological framework gained significant traction in the United States, largely due to the efforts of the Dallas Theological Seminary, which became its main institution of education and advocacy. A pivotal moment in the propagation of dispensationalist thought came with the publication of the Scofield Reference Bible in 1909. This edition not only featured the biblical text but also included extensive study notes authored by C. I. Scofield. These notes were instrumental in interpreting the Scriptures through a dispensationalist lens, effectively guiding readers in an easy-to-follow style.[1]

The Dallas Theological Seminary, established in 1924 by the influential theologian Lewis Sperry Chafer, has long stood as a premier institution for theological education. From its founding, the seminary has played a pivotal role in educating, promoting, and safeguarding the principles of dispensationalism. Through the dedicated efforts of its esteemed teachers, influential writers, committed missionaries, and many prominent pastors associated with the dispensational movement, the institution has significantly impacted the landscape of American Evangelicalism. Their robust theological framework, characterized by a dynamic approach to biblical interpretation, has not only shaped the faith of countless individuals but also fueled an energetic outreach that resonates across America. The seminary's influence can be felt in the teachings and practices of numerous congregations, cementing its status as a cornerstone of dispensational thought.

A seminal work in this field is *Dispensationalism Today*, authored by Charles C. Ryrie and published in 1965 by the Moody Bible Institute. This book is widely revered as one of the most comprehensive books on dispensationalism, earning Ryrie considerable acclaim. Throughout his prolific career, Ryrie authored over two dozen books, becoming a skilled apologist and a highly regarded speaker and educator. His influence extends beyond his supporters; even those who vehemently disagree with his views recognize the significant impact he has had on American religious thought. Ryrie's work has undeniably shaped the trajectory of popular Christianity and dispensationalism.

Dr. Charles C. Ryrie (1925–2016) was a prominent theologian who claimed that his beliefs were firmly rooted in a literal interpretation of the Bible. He maintained that biblical passages should be understood plainly, avoiding the tendency to spiritualize those that do not present themselves

---

1. Gregg, "Is Dispensationalism Indispensable?"

clearly as metaphorical. Despite his stated dedication to this theological approach, certain critics have raised concerns about his commitment to literalism. They argue that his contemporary interpretations of the Bible, which lean towards a modernistic perspective, appear to clash with his principle of literalism. This tension between stated literalism and interpretative methods is explicit throughout dispensationalism, with critics claiming that dispensationalists "spiritualize history and literalize prophecy."[2]

Many of you are likely well-acquainted with the tenets of dispensationalist theology, so a brief overview should suffice to highlight its key features. Dispensationalism is perhaps most recognized for its unique eschatological views, particularly the doctrine surrounding the pre-tribulation rapture of the church.

This doctrine posits that the current age of the church will transition into a seven-year period of intense tribulation. Significantly, before this tribulation period commences—hence the term "pre-tribulation"—believers in Christ will be taken up to heaven in what is often referred to as the rapture. During this time, these individuals will dwell in the presence of Christ until his anticipated second coming, which occurs at the culmination of the tribulation.

When the anticipated second coming occurs, the redeemed—those who have been saved and transformed—will return to earth in the company of Christ. This momentous event heralds the establishment of his millennial kingdom, a period of a thousand years marked by peace and divine governance. Notably, those who adhere to dispensationalism not only subscribe to this rapture perspective but also align themselves with premillennialism. They hold a steadfast conviction that Christ will exercise his sovereignty on earth in a concrete and visible way throughout this millennium. This belief implies a future where his reign is not only spiritual but also manifests in a physical presence, transforming the world in palpable ways during this significant period.

Dispensationalism and Reformed covenant theology, commonly associated with Calvinism, differ in several key aspects, with one notable distinction being their understanding of the concept of the "people of God." Covenant theology suggests that there is one unified people of God, emphasizing continuity between the Old Testament Israelites and the New Testament believers in Christ. In this view, the promises and purposes of God remain consistent throughout Scripture, unifying all who are in faith.

---

2. Gerstner, *Wrongly Dividing*, 81.

This conflict, however, does not hinder a few Calvinist churches from embracing some dispensational beliefs as well.

In contrast to traditional Reformed covenant theology, dispensationalism introduces a more segmented perspective, particularly regarding eschatology—the study of end times. Dispensationalists assert a clear distinction between Israel and the church, arguing that these two groups have separate roles in God's divine plan. They maintain that Israel is integral to the timing and unfolding of end-time events, believing that after the event known as the rapture—where the church is taken up to be with Christ—God will resume his specific dealings with Israel apart from the church. This dualistic approach highlights the belief that God's promises to Israel remain active and significant in the overall narrative of salvation history, indicating a future for the nation that is distinct from the church.

Dispensationalism views the establishment of Israel in 1948 as a crucial turning point in the timeline of prophetic history. Adherents of this theological perspective have long held the belief that the reestablishment of Israel as a sovereign nation would occur before significant end-time events unfold. Central to dispensational eschatology is the geographic region of Israel, which not only serves as a focal point for prophecy but also garners fervent support from many Christian Evangelicals. This strong backing reflects a deep conviction among these believers that the nation's significance extends beyond mere political developments, intertwining with their understanding of biblical prophecy and the anticipated return of Christ.

With that cursory background, we can delve into the relationship between dispensationalism and the themes presented in this book. The late John Gerstner, a distinguished theologian and scholar, offered a thorough and insightful critique of dispensationalism in his seminal 1991 work, *Wrongly Dividing the Word of Truth*. His thoroughness and expertise shine through the pages, constructing arguments that are both detailed and compelling. One of the most striking aspects of the book is found in the final hundred pages, where Gerstner confidently extends an invitation to several prominent dispensationalists. In this engaging segment, he encourages them to share their insights and perspectives regarding his critiques, fostering a dynamic exchange of ideas. Gerstner's responses to their contributions are disseminated throughout that section of his book, weaving together a vibrant dialogue that significantly enhances the depth and thoroughness of the work. This interplay not only sheds light on differing viewpoints but also showcases the complexities of the subject matter, making for a compelling conclusion.

While I'm neither a Calvinist nor a dispensationalist, I've gained considerable insight into dispensationalism due to its widespread influence in my part of Southern California. In addition, my trips to Israel in 1998 and 2000 were both led by dispensational leaders. Apart from myself on the first trip and my daughter and me on the second, nearly all the other participants in the groups were dispensationalists. The conversations and discussions I had with these leaders in Israel, as well as with many knowledgeable dispensationalists back home, have deepened my understanding of the areas where our beliefs diverge.

In this chapter, I will reference Dr. Gerstner's insights as he expresses ideas that I have personally embraced for many decades. His eloquence brings clarity to the perspectives I have struggled to articulate, making his words resonate more profoundly than my own ever could.

Dispensationalism encompasses a wide range of beliefs, but for the purpose of this book, I will focus on its antinomianism. Dispensational antinomianism is closely tied to easy-believism and its false sense of security regarding salvation. There are various definitions of antinomianism, ranging from overly polite and vague to brutally honest and strikingly revealing. Below are a few of those definitions.

On the vanilla side, Webster's dictionary defines an antinomian as "one who holds that under the gospel dispensation of grace, the moral law is of no use or obligation because faith alone is necessary to salvation."[3]

Webster's dictionary defines antinomianism by highlighting the "dispensation of grace," which is one of the seven distinct periods in church history uniquely taught by dispensationalists. Right from the start, even this neutral, secular one-sentence definition connects antinomianism with dispensationalism, illustrating a clear relationship between the two.

But as we dive a little deeper, we reach the next layer with this online definition by Ligonier Ministries: "Antinomianism says that God does not require a believer to obey the moral law (i.e., the Ten Commandments). In its more extreme and perverted form, antinomianism permits immoral behavior based on the leniency of grace."[4] It goes on to say,

---

3. *Merriam-Webster*, s. v. "antinomian," https://www.merriam-webster.com/dictionary/antinomianism.

4. Ligonier Editorial, "Legalism and Antinomianism?"

FAKE SALVATION IN MODERN GNOSTIC AMERICA

> In the early church, certain false teachers promoted the idea that God's grace tolerates lawless living (see 2 Peter and Jude). Some wickedly dismissed sexual immorality in the name of grace (Jude 4). The Apostle John contended against antinomian ideas in his first letter (1 John 2:4).
>
> Throughout church history, antinomianism has appeared in less overt and perverse forms than that in which it appeared in the early church. Martin Luther wrote *Against the Antinomians* to refute the erroneous teaching of the neo-Lutheran antinomian Johannes Agricola. . . . In the twentieth century, notable dispensational teachers promoted a form of antinomianism called "easy-believism."
>
> Antinomianism works on people's consciences by convincing them that God does not require us to turn from our wicked ways. Antinomianism presents a Christianity that requires no personal effort or spiritual striving against sin. It offers a counterfeit freedom to the true freedom that Christ gives believers.[5]

The above definition is starting to display a little more substance because it accurately links together antinomianism, dispensationalism, and easy-believism. They are explicitly describing dispensational antinomianism when referring to the type of "Christianity that requires no personal effort or spiritual striving against sin."

As we go even deeper, the following definition by Tim Pietz makes a very interesting connection:

> Martin Luther coined the term "Antinomianism" to confront a resurgence of the heresy. "By grace alone" and "through faith alone" were two foundational truths Luther proclaimed—but one of Luther's collaborators, Johann Agricola, wondered if that might be taken a little further. If legalism was the problem, and grace was the solution, wouldn't it make sense to stop preaching about commands like the Ten Commandments? Those were Old Testament laws, wiped away by Christ's sacrifice, weren't they? Sin was no longer a problem because it was all forgiven. Agricola may not have realized, but his position was strikingly similar to the beliefs of [the second-century Gnostic] Marcion.[6]

Yes, Tim Pietz notes that antinomian beliefs are essentially the same as second-century gnostic beliefs. In earlier chapters, I mentioned Valentinian

---

5. Ligonier Editorial, "Legalism and Antinomianism?"
6. Pietz, "Antinomianism."

Gnosticism because we have their actual writings, thanks to the 1945 discovery of the Nag Hammadi library. However, the Gnosticism of Marcion was also prevalent in the second century, and I devote half a chapter to him in my book *The Battle for the Divinity of Christ in the Early Centuries*.

The following series of quotations from Dr. John Gerstner display a profound comprehension of the issues associated with dispensationalism. Interestingly, he reveals in the preface of his book titled *Wrongly Dividing the Word of Truth* and in other places that he was once a dispensationalist, which lends a unique perspective to his critiques. His journey from adherence to scrutiny enriches the discussion and adds depth to the exploration of these critical theological themes.

Gerstner infers that dispensationalism is essentially a form of modern American Gnosticism:

> The dispensationalist tends to conceive of faith as intellectual fact. He recognizes himself to be a sinner and Christ to be the proffered Savior and believing that fact he is thereby justified.[7]

In chapter 2, we explored the fundamental essence of Gnosticism, which is rooted in the belief that true salvation comes from acquiring intellectual knowledge, often referred to as "the knowledge that saves."[8] This knowledge is seen as the crucial and unique key needed to unlock the door to guaranteed salvation for each person. Interestingly, while Gerstner describes that key feature of Gnosticism when he speaks of believing that "intellectual fact," he does not use the term *gnostic*; instead, he refers to dispensationalism.

In the quotes that follow, Gerstner solidly links dispensationalism and antinomianism. In fact, that is the key issue he opposes regarding dispensationalism. The concept of antinomianism is intrinsically linked to the modern theological framework of dispensationalism; discussing one inevitably leads to a consideration of the other. This inseparable bond becomes particularly evident when examining the historical and doctrinal developments of dispensationalism. Recently, however, a notable trend has emerged among some dispensationalists who are attempting to distance themselves from this long-standing association. Nevertheless, this effort is largely in vain. They cannot be separated, as Gerstner's reason for leaving dispensationalism makes clear.

---

7. Gerstner, *Wrongly Dividing*, 225.
8. Lee, *Against the Protestant Gnostics*, 55.

Gerstner was a dispensationalist until Ryrie's position on anti-Lordship "brought home to [him] the realization that contemporary dispensationalism like past dispensationalism is still committed to the nonnegotiable doctrine of antinomianism."[9]

I will reference Charles Ryrie throughout this chapter because he was widely recognized among dispensationalists and others as one of the clearest and most articulate writers in the field. His works are characterized by a straightforward and accessible style.

Ryrie boldly confronts complex issues with remarkable clarity, unlike many dispensational authors who tend to sidestep or obscure them. His writing demonstrates a genuine willingness to directly engage with challenging topics, making his contributions both valuable and thought-provoking. The following is an example of that clarity from his book *Balancing the Christian Life*:

> The importance of this question cannot be overestimated in relation to both salvation and sanctification. The message of faith only and the message of faith plus commitment of life cannot both be the gospel; therefore, one of them is false and comes under the curse of perverting the gospel or preaching another gospel.[10]

While many are now trying to distance themselves from this point, and some dispensationalists even try to claim it was never part of their belief system, Ryrie is unmistakably clear about the core principles of dispensational antinomianism. He articulates the message as it has been expressed since the days of Darby: your profession of faith is what saves you. That is, in essence, the gospel of dispensationalism. From the very start, dispensationalism has maintained that adding anything of your own to your salvation undermines Christ's completed work. Any additions are seen as works, and by insisting on them, you are essentially seeking salvation through your own merits. They argue that these Protestant works echo the flawed system of meritocracy in Catholic works. After all, isn't that what the Reformation was all about?

Ryrie's stance is clear: "Faith only!" He then contrasts this with what he terms "commitment of life," which pertains to your behavior, and according to dispensationalism, any modification toward holiness, or more

---

9. Gerstner, *Wrongly Dividing*, xi.
10. Ryrie, *Balancing the Christian Life*, 170.

Christian living, or cleaning up your act, or any kind of "commitment of life" is "perverting the gospel."

A former president of Grace Theological Seminary, Alva MacLean, uses the same dispensational logic as Ryrie in an attempt to show that the Bible teaches antinomianism:

> Alva McLean (one of the editors of the Scofield Reference Bible) argues that "under the law" could only have one of two meanings. Either it referred to being under the law as the basis of salvation or as a way of life. Since no one was ever saved by keeping the law, the former possibility is excluded, and the expression can only refer to being under the law as a way of life. So, when Romans 6:14 says that the Christian is not under the law, it means that he is free of it as a way of life.[11]

Gerstner writes that Scofield was equally clear:

> [According to Scofield, noted in the Scofield Bible], "The Christian's disobedience does not affect his salvation." One can see from Scofield's note that [the dispensationalist's] salvation is an accomplished fact because he once professed faith in Christ. It is obvious that one could go on lying, blaspheming, fornicating, and murdering for a lifetime with no threat to one's salvation.[12]

> [Scofield] emphatically and dogmatically teaches that a Christian may be carnal all his life and yet be a Christian. These statements alone—and his writings are full of statements like them—would prove that America's most famous and influential dispensationalist was an arch antinomian.[13]

Moreover, Gerstner goes on to say,

> All traditional dispensationalists teach that converted Christian persons can live in sin throughout their post-conversion lives with no threat to their eternal destiny. This [is] fatal antinomianism, the denial of the relevance of the moral law to true Christians.

> [In dispensationalism] the condition of [being a] carnal Christian [is] a normal state of affairs [and they may remain so] all of their earthly lives.[14]

---

11. Gerstner, *Wrongly Dividing*, 208.
12. Gerstner, *Wrongly Dividing*, 207.
13. Gerstner, *Wrongly Dividing*, 207.
14. Gerstner, *Wrongly Dividing*, 201, 138.

Charles Ryrie adds the following as part of the dispensational eternal security argument:

> Normally, one who has believed can be described as a believer; that is, one who continues to believe. But a believer may come to the place of not believing, and yet God will not disown him, since He cannot disown himself.[15]

In their book *Major Bible Themes*, Lewis Sperry Chafer, the founder of the Dallas Theological Seminary, and John Walvoord, one of its past presidents, said,

> A carnal Christian is as perfectly saved as a spiritual Christian; for no experience, or merit, or service can form any part of the grounds of salvation.[16]

And, again, Gerstner says,

> Both Ryrie and [another noted dispensationalist], Hodges, agree that a person's faith can totally die, and he will still possess eternal life.[17]

John Gerstner sums up all of the above when saying,

> If total Christian carnality is a possibility, antinomianism is a certainty.[18]

The concept of antinomianism is deeply woven into the structure of dispensationalism, revealing a consistent relationship between the two. This connection is evident even in the absence of the aforementioned quotes. Pastors have been giving assurances of guaranteed salvation to individuals—virtually all of whom they have never met—through the airwaves, during altar calls, or in massive stadium gatherings. This practice explicitly proclaims that a mere verbal profession of faith serves as a passport to eternity, providing a sense of security with the assertion that all aspects of one's life and behavior fall under the protective cover of Christ's sacrifice.

Every person in the listening audience is informed that all they need to do is join the pastor in the sinner's prayer, acknowledge that they are unworthy, and then state that they have faith in Christ and his finished work

---

15. Gerstner, *Wrongly Dividing*, 212.
16. Chafer and Walvoord, *Major Bible Themes*, 214.
17. Gerstner, *Wrongly Dividing*, 221.
18. Gerstner, *Wrongly Dividing*, 210.

PAINTED INTO A CORNER: DISPENSATIONALISM

on the cross. Then, according to dispensationalism, they can go out and live the exact same life as they lived before, or they can choose to live any other type of lifestyle they wish with no fear of losing their salvation. Other than the verbal profession of faith they have made, dispensationalism teaches that there are no behavioral qualifications or conditions at all. Salvation being granted over the airwaves, during altar calls, or in massive stadium gatherings is obviously a blanket offer or blanket call.

What are some common examples of blanket offers that many of us recognize and encounter in our daily lives? A television or radio commercial that encourages viewers to enter a specific code for a 20 percent discount serves as a classic example of a blanket offer, extending the invitation to all who tune in. Similarly, a concert where attendees are encouraged to mention the DJ's name for a 10 percent discount on concert merchandise exemplifies the same kind of broad marketing strategy, aiming to engage a wide audience without any restrictions.

A great example of a blanket offer can be seen with a baseball team that hands out rally towels to every fan as they enter the stadium for home playoff games. Regardless of their personal circumstances, such as individual behavior or lifestyle choices, every attendee receives a towel, ensuring everyone is treated equally and welcomed into the exciting atmosphere of the event.

In contrast, the following are examples of conditional offers that most of us would recognize. For instance, an employer might extend a job offer to a candidate with the stipulation that they successfully pass a comprehensive criminal background check and complete employment verification. In the academic realm, a university might grant provisional admission to a prospective student, but only if they achieve a specified GPA or standardized test score by the time the academic term begins. In a similar vein, a hospital might extend an offer for a brain surgeon position to a qualified candidate. This would typically require the individual to hold a valid medical license, have earned a relevant degree in neurosurgery or a related field, and demonstrate the necessary hands-on experience in performing complex brain surgeries.

Conditional offers are designed to become valid solely when certain predetermined standards or criteria are successfully met. These offers are tailored for distinct individuals who possess unique qualifications and skills, making them highly specific in nature. Conversely, blanket offers are inclusive and extend to all individuals within the audience, regardless of their particular qualifications or background.

When any individual who was within earshot of the secular blanket call arrives to claim their promise, they cannot be turned away or disqualified based on their behavior or lifestyle. This means that even if someone is recognized as the notorious hit man from the latest episode of *America's Most Wanted*, or if they happen to be the prostitute who was hired for an evening of group debauchery at last night's bachelor party, or even if they were just seen on the news being sentenced for child molestation, it does not matter. The blanket announcement is universally applicable to all who heard it, regardless of their personal history or choices. Everyone is treated equally under the terms of the call, no matter how controversial their behavior or lifestyle may be.

It's the same with the blanket dispensational call, giving away salvation—whether broadcast over the airwaves, during altar calls, or at massive stadium gatherings. This call is undeniably a broad announcement aimed at everyone within earshot, effectively casting a wide net to embrace all individuals present. The implication is clear—every person in the audience is eligible for what is heralded as an irrevocable guarantee of salvation, irrespective of their personal conduct or lifestyle choices.

It resembles the television or radio commercial, except that the "code" one has to enter is the "sinner's prayer." Similarly, it echoes the concert where merely mentioning the name "DJ Jesus" suffices. And like the baseball stadium, you're entitled to a free heavenly towel because Jesus wiped away your sins.

When any individual who was within earshot of the dispensational pastor's blanket call "arrives" to claim their promised salvation, they cannot be turned away or disqualified based on their behavior or lifestyle. This means that even if the Christian convert is recognized as that notorious hit man, or if they happen to be that bachelor party prostitute, or even if they were the child molester just seen on TV, it does not matter. The blanket announcement is universally applicable to all who heard it, regardless of their personal history or choices. Everyone is treated equally under the terms of the call, no matter how controversial their behavior or lifestyle may be.

All television and radio assurances, along with the guarantees of salvation offered through altar calls, bear witness to this crucial fact: none of these pastors would be handing out these blanket assurances of salvation if they were not thoroughly committed to antinomianism. This insight not only encapsulates the profound ideas presented by Dietrich Bonhoeffer but also highlights his argument effectively. It is nearly impossible for the concept of "cheap grace" to get any cheaper than when it is handed out with the same casual indifference and universal availability as free towels at a baseball stadium.

As previously indicated, offers of salvation can generally be categorized as either blanket or conditional. The salvific messages communicated through various mediums, including radio broadcasts, altar calls during church services, and large-scale gatherings in venues such as baseball stadiums, have historically fallen under the category of blanket offers. Consistent with the core tenets of dispensationalism, these offers have often carried an antinomian perspective, suggesting that an individual's behavior and moral conduct are irrelevant to the assurance of salvation they provide.

However, a recent development suggests that these pastors are now promoting a hybrid model of salvation that incorporates both blanket and conditional aspects. They still extend a broad invitation; otherwise, they could not offer guaranteed salvation to individuals they have never met or assessed during public events. However, they are now adding an implicit understanding that certain conditions may apply. This evolving approach raises questions about the nature of these offers and the theological implications surrounding them, particularly in the context of their previously established beliefs.

For at least half a century, individuals like myself have been urging them to acknowledge the truths that they are only just beginning to see. It raises a question: What ultimately led to this realization? What specific illumination from the Holy Spirit allowed them to truly open their eyes and perceive what had consistently eluded them?

In reality, their profound realization had less to do with the Holy Spirit and more to do with the unholy culture that has infiltrated both the clergy and the church. As they stood by, witnessing the massive wildfire consuming the very essence of traditional Christianity, the towering flames clearly illuminated the scene for them. They could finally see the truth: the homosexual revolution brought home to them the point that dispensationalism is wrong and that behavior does matter in biblical Christianity.

A significant number of churches are grappling with profound divisions surrounding this issue, prompting them to critically reassess their long-standing beliefs. Specifically, many are now willing to take a fresh look at the entire concept of dispensationalism. This context makes the release of this book especially relevant and timely, as it arrives at a moment when many congregations are finally willing to put aside dispensational dogmatism and consider other perspectives. For many, it represents a moment of awakening, as congregations are increasingly willing to confront their long-standing views—especially concerning the antinomian tendencies inherent in dispensationalism. Many pastors who have traditionally supported the core tenets of dispensationalism, which espouse the idea that individuals are free to live without moral constraints, are now unexpectedly discovering that they have inadvertently taken a stand with what is clearly the wrong side.

Pastors found themselves in a dilemma. A significant portion of their congregation, disillusioned by the deviant behaviors and lifestyles exhibited by certain pastors and members, has decided to leave the church. Meanwhile, the remaining congregation holds steadfast to the teachings that these dispensational pastors have imparted throughout their lives. They strongly believe that "a carnal Christian is as perfectly saved as a spiritual Christian,"[19] a conviction that complicates matters for the pastors.

These pastors now face the repercussions of their own teachings, which have facilitated the emergence of the deviant lifestyle group within the church community. This situation is not just a coincidence but rather the direct result of a slippery slope that they initiated decades ago. It represents the culmination of the various dispensational doctrines and beliefs they have steadfastly endorsed during the entirety of their ministerial careers, which uncomfortably leaves them on the side of the homosexual half of the church, leading them to hastily try to address the issue by attempting to place a Band-Aid over a deep, festering wound.

This scenario has shed light on a long-standing concern raised by critics of dispensationalism: it appears that dispensationalists required the emergence of a troubling cultural backdrop within the church to fully grasp the detrimental environment they have inadvertently fostered and permitted to infiltrate their sacred space. Perhaps the sight of a drag queen pastor guaranteeing salvation to an entire drag queen congregation shockingly awakened them from their conformist dispensational slumber?

What was the makeshift solution dispensational pastors hurriedly stitched together to mask the gaping wound? In a rushed attempt to patch things up, they proposed a solitary condition to attach to the blanket assurance of salvation they have been peddling for decades, all the while hoping

---

19. Gerstner, *Wrongly Dividing*, 210.

that we would not think too deeply about their alterations. They still identified as dispensationalists, yet they made the decision to rescind the "lifestyle doesn't matter" exemption, but exclusively for one group: homosexuals.

I'm obviously not advocating for homosexual inclusion within any aspect of the church; rather, I am highlighting a glaring inconsistency. Many dispensational pastors now urge their congregations to put aside much of what they have been taught about dispensationalism throughout their entire church lives. These pastors seem to expect everyone to disregard their grasp of the English language, unlearn what they've been taught, and acquiesce to the pastor's new convoluted and self-contradictory rhetoric.

It is telling that, in the past, opponents of dispensationalism were often labeled as naive or simplistic individuals who couldn't grasp the straightforward messages conveyed in the Bible. For instance, they were made to feel inadequate in their inability to understand even the most direct Scriptures, such as 1 John 5:13, which explicitly states, "That ye may know that ye have eternal life." The insistence was that opponents of dispensationalism were somehow missing the obvious meaning of such passages and were often chastised for their supposed lack of comprehension.

However, for the moment, let's revisit and list the key elements surrounding the assertions made about dispensationalism. This brief overview aims to shed light on the significant differences between the earlier unconditional dispensational teachings regarding salvation and the more recent single-condition teachings that have emerged. Historically, unconditional dispensationalism posits that salvation is granted solely by grace and cannot be influenced by human actions or decisions. In contrast, the newer conditional teachings suggest that specific conditions may be disqualifying, but only for one group.

1. "The message of faith only and the message of faith plus commitment of life cannot both be the gospel."[20]

    STILL APPLIES to heterosexual dispensational listeners but DOES NOT APPLY to homosexual dispensational listeners.

2. "Your profession of faith is what saves you. . . . Any additions are seen as works, and by insisting on them, you are essentially seeking salvation through your own merits."[21]

---

20. Ryrie, *Balancing the Christian Life*, 170.
21. See p. 40.

FAKE SALVATION IN MODERN GNOSTIC AMERICA

STILL APPLIES to heterosexual dispensational listeners but DOES NOT APPLY to homosexual dispensational listeners.

3. "Alva McLean (one of the editors of the Scofield Reference Bible) argues that 'under the law' could only have one of two meanings. Either it referred to being under the law as the basis of salvation or as a way of life. Since no one was ever saved by keeping the law, the former possibility is excluded, and the expression can only refer to being under the law as a way of life."[22]

   STILL APPLIES to heterosexual dispensational listeners but DOES NOT APPLY to homosexual dispensational listeners.

4. "[According to Scofield, noted in the Scofield Bible], 'The Christian's disobedience does not affect his salvation.' One can see from Scofield's note that [the dispensationalist's] salvation is an accomplished fact because he once professed faith in Christ. It is obvious that one could go on lying, blaspheming, fornicating, and murdering for a lifetime with no threat to one's salvation."[23]

   STILL APPLIES to heterosexual dispensational listeners but DOES NOT APPLY to homosexual dispensational listeners.

5. "[Scofield] emphatically and dogmatically teaches that a Christian may be carnal all his life."[24]

   STILL APPLIES to heterosexual dispensational listeners but DOES NOT APPLY to homosexual dispensational listeners.

6. "All traditional dispensationalists teach that converted Christian persons can live in sin throughout their post-conversion lives with no threat to their eternal destiny."[25]

   STILL APPLIES to heterosexual dispensational listeners but DOES NOT APPLY to homosexual dispensational listeners.

---

22. Gerstner, *Wrongly Dividing*, 208.
23. Gerstner, *Wrongly Dividing*, 207.
24. Gerstner, *Wrongly Dividing*, 207.
25. Gerstner, *Wrongly Dividing*, 201.

7. "Normally, one who has believed can be described as a believer; that is, one who continues to believe. But a believer may come to the place of not believing, and yet God will not disown him, since He cannot disown himself."[26]

   STILL APPLIES to heterosexual dispensational listeners but DOES NOT APPLY to homosexual dispensational listeners.

8. "A carnal Christian is as perfectly saved as a spiritual Christian; for no experience or merit or service can form any part of the grounds of salvation."[27]

   STILL APPLIES to heterosexual dispensational listeners but DOES NOT APPLY to homosexual dispensational listeners.

9. "Both Ryrie and Hodges agree that a person's faith can totally die, and he will still possess eternal life."[28]

   STILL APPLIES to heterosexual dispensational listeners but DOES NOT APPLY to homosexual dispensational listeners.

The issue at hand is quite clear. Dispensationalists find themselves in a bind, unable to reconcile these contradictions. The dispensational call is either a blanket offer or a conditional offer—it's one or the other. They now face the reality that behavior does play a role, but only for certain individuals. This puts them in a difficult and hypocritical position, as they must claim that the blood of Christ covers all heterosexual behaviors while excluding all homosexual behaviors. That is an impossible circle to square.

Why can't these pastors just say that conditional salvation based on sexually deviant behaviors includes all non-biblical sexual behaviors, heterosexual or homosexual (which is what the critics of dispensationalism have been saying all along)? They can't. The one condition they have now imposed makes clear that they've been handing out fake salvation to homosexuals for almost two centuries. But because the culture had not embraced that behavior and much of it was underground, that blight on Christianity was hidden. Now, it's a glaring, festering sore that's dividing and destroying long-standing churches.

---

26. Gerstner, *Wrongly Dividing*, 212.
27. Chafer and Walvoord, *Major Bible Themes*, 214.
28. Gerstner, *Wrongly Dividing*, 221.

As a result of this issue, many individuals are reexamining their Bibles after feeling compelled to leave their long-established churches. These churches, once steadfast in their beliefs, have begun to conform to societal pressures, allowing what was once hidden to become widely accepted and, in some circles, almost sacred. Others may even find themselves more open to Gerstner's perspectives, especially now that dispensational pastors are significantly altering the tenets of dispensationalism themselves. As Gerstner said, "No matter how many other important truths it proclaims [dispensationalism] cannot be called Christian if it empties Christianity of its essential message. It's as serious as that."[29]

We know that this is a drastic alteration that these pastors are making. Either behavior does not matter, as it's been in dispensationalism for two hundred years, or behavior does matter, as is being presented now for basically one issue. But they cannot have it both ways. Behavior is important; it either matters or it doesn't—there's no in-between.

For two hundred years, the blanket call included homosexuals, which assured them that they would one day stand before God, remind him that their dispensational pastor had awarded them irrevocable salvation, and God would agree. Now, dispensational pastors are retroactively admitting that was all a fraud.

After all, if it was invalid for homosexual listeners, that means it was invalid for every listener. Nowhere in the Bible is it even implied that God will overlook heterosexual sexual sin while at the same time disqualifying people based on homosexual sexual sin. It was fake salvation all along for every listener. If you took it as legitimate, you have been thoroughly deceived, even though Christ warned us against being deceived. "It is folly for anyone to imagine that man can set the requirements for salvation and impose them upon God."[30]

Why don't pastors simply put an end to the guarantees of television salvation, radio salvation, altar call salvation, and stadium salvation? They can't do this because by honestly admitting that their promises of salvation hold no weight with God, they would undermine the entire dispensational business model. Such a confession would reveal that the whole system is a scam, and if one of them were candid with their congregation, the members would likely just go down the street and join a less scrupulous church where the pastor is still handing out fake promises of salvation.

---

29. Gerstner, *Wrongly Dividing*, 142.
30. Hunt, *What Love Is This?*, 205.

PAINTED INTO A CORNER: DISPENSATIONALISM

But for now, one thing is obvious: modern dispensationalists have painted themselves into a corner.

As we approach the conclusion of this chapter, let us take a moment to clarify the essential dispensational distinction between standing and state. This distinction is not merely a theoretical one; it plays a critical role in understanding the indispensable relationship between standing and state within the framework of dispensational theology.

As Gerstner explains,

> [Dispensationalism draws a] distinction between standing and state. At his so-called "new birth," nothing in [his] nature changes. His standing, which is his legal relationship to God, is supposed to change. His state, which is his own condition, does not necessarily change at the time or even thereafter. [While] the Spirit indwells the person, the old fallen nature remains untouched by the Holy Spirit.
>
> The person is not changed; he is counterbalanced. Dispensationalists [teach] that the Christian need not forsake sin. This gives rise to the dispensational doctrine of the two kinds of Christians, the spiritual and the carnal. The carnal dispensationalist Christian [can continue] to be controlled by his old nature all his life.[31]

At the core of dispensationalism are the concepts of state and standing, which, while seemingly straightforward, carry profound implications. The essential notion is that when one makes a conscious decision for Christ through the airwaves or altar call, their standing before God is transformed. This change signifies a new status in a spiritual sense, indicating that they are now seen as righteous in the eyes of God. However, it is crucial to understand that this shift in standing does not automatically alter one's state—referring to their actions and behavior—which may remain largely the same. This distinction highlights the complex relationship between a person's spiritual identity and their everyday conduct. As explained below,

> A man's standing is perfect before God, though his state may not be. Justification in dispensationalism is [by] knowledge. This turns out to be an instantaneous event.
>
> Lewis Sperry Chafer [said that] claiming the blessing is all there is to it.[32]

---

31. Gerstner, *Wrongly Dividing*, 204, 205.
32. Gerstner, *Wrongly Dividing*, 231, 232.

FAKE SALVATION IN MODERN GNOSTIC AMERICA

In the framework of dispensationalism, there is a pivotal moment that often occurs when an individual prays for salvation while watching a religious broadcast or walks to the front of a church or stadium during an altar call. At this instant, dispensationalists believe that the person experiences immediate justification, leading to a perfect standing before God from that moment onward. This profound transformation in spiritual status does not necessarily correspond with any visible change in the person's behavior or actions. The core requirement is simply acknowledging what Jesus accomplished on the cross. As theologian Lewis Sperry Chafer articulated, the act of claiming this divine blessing is all that is needed to secure one's spiritual state, regardless of the ongoing realities of daily life.

Saving knowledge is involved, which is obviously gnostic. The fact that behavior doesn't change makes it textbook antinomianism—definitively confirming that moral laws, behavior, or lifestyle do not matter. Furthermore, the dispensationalist viewpoint asserts that a person's standing before God is changed instantaneously simply by proclaiming a particular blessing. This notion makes salvation accessible to everyone within hearing distance without any prerequisites or limitations. The way one chooses to walk as a Christian then becomes entirely inconsequential in this context, paving the way for anyone to respond to this message. Dispensationalism imposes no conditions or limitations on your Christian walk or lifestyle:

> John Nelson Darby taught this antinomianism in its crudest form. He was once asked about 1 John 1:7 ("But if we walk in the light . . ."). He explained that the text deals with where you walk, not how you walk. [Darby was] asked further, "Suppose a real Christian turned his back on the light [walked away from Christ] deliberately and permanently?" Without hesitation, Darby replied, "Then the light would shine upon his back."[33]

Turning your back on the light and yet still finding salvation represents a profound departure from any sense of obligatory Christian behavior. You're not even obligated to be a Christian; how can there be any obligation to adhere to any Christian behavior? This statement reflects a clear and unequivocal understanding of dispensationalism as it has traditionally been interpreted and taught. There are no prerequisite conditions for transitioning from a state of spiritual death to one of spiritual life. Every individual, without exception, is invited to cross the bridge of dispensational antinomianism.

33. Gerstner, *Wrongly Dividing*, 206.

PAINTED INTO A CORNER: DISPENSATIONALISM

The phrase "Where you walk, not how you walk" resonates as a recurring theme in Darby's dispensationalist writings, illustrating a perspective that has endured across two centuries of dispensational thought. This idea is undeniably reflected in contemporary American Protestant churches where, in practice, the call remains a blanket call in spite of pastors attempting to backfill the vintage dispensational landscape with subterfuge.

CHAPTER 5

SHOW ME A PICTURE

You've probably run across various retellings of the story about the four blind men who each touch different parts of an elephant only to describe it based on their limited experience with what they feel. The first blind man touches the elephant's side and declares it feels like a wall. The second blind man runs his hands over the trunk and compares it to a snake. The third, feeling the tusk, insists it resembles a spear, while the fourth, who touches the leg, confidently states it feels like a tree. Each blind man believes he has the whole picture, unaware that their perspectives are shaped by their singular experiences.

Much like the proverbial elephant, examining individual aspects of modern Gnosticism can present a skewed image of the whole. That's because modern Gnosticism embodies an overabundance of beliefs, doctrines, and cultural influences, rendering it both enigmatic and intricate. That being said, let's begin with a short list of prominent outward characteristics that will lay the foundation for later clarification.

1. Throughout history, proponents of Gnosticism have always used the Bible to support their beliefs, creating the impression that their interpretations offer the only true understanding of Scripture. Consequently, modern Gnosticism does the same, presenting itself in a manner that seems more aligned with the essence of biblical truth than any competing theology.

2. The teachings and beliefs often resonate deeply with the themes and mysteries found in the Bible, giving the impression that they capture

the essence of spiritual understanding more clearly than any other historical or contemporary interpretations of Scripture. After absorbing the sequential gnostic line of reasoning without opposing views, the listeners develop a sense of elitist enlightenment, leaving them with the conviction that all others have been deceived.

3. The allure has consistently been, and continues to be, captivating and incredibly compelling. Within a remarkably brief period, individuals find themselves convinced that they have a personal relationship with God, believing they are part of the only authentic expression of biblical Christianity. The emotional and seductive nature of Gnosticism often leads individuals to unconsciously relinquish their unique identities in favor of a shared gnostic identity, profoundly transforming their sense of self. The transformation is powerful, fostering a deep sense of belonging, purpose, exclusivity, and unwavering conviction.

4. The gnostic guarantee of salvation has consistently captivated individuals throughout history, possessing a compelling allure that draws even the most skeptical minds into its embrace. This enticing doctrine provides a sense of certainty and assurance that strongly resonates with our inherent self-centeredness. As a result, many people—who might question or challenge beliefs in other aspects of their lives—find themselves willingly accepting the teachings presented to them, often without reservation. This acceptance is driven not by logic or evidence but by a profound alignment with their personal yearnings and hopes.

5. These groups often make a concerted effort to distinguish themselves from others, with the perception that everyone outside their circle is disconnected from the truth. By adopting unique beliefs, practices, and narratives, they create a strong sense of identity that reinforces their convictions while simultaneously casting doubt on the validity of alternative perspectives. This effort not only highlights their differences but also deepens the illusion that they alone possess an exclusive understanding of reality.

The above verbal description may lack the clarity that a photograph can provide. To illustrate the point more vividly, consider the following image:

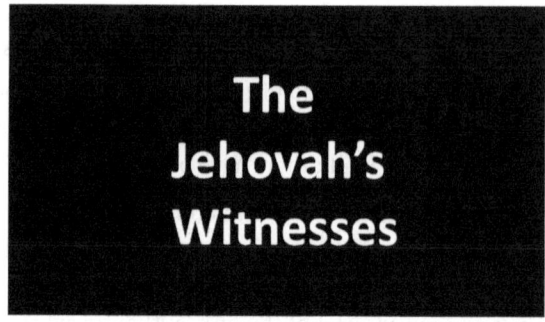

The Jehovah's Witnesses are widely acknowledged for their distortion of traditional Christian teachings, deliberately fueling a sense of pride among their followers through counterfeit scholarship and fake guarantees of exclusive salvation. They also provide a clear and relatable illustration of modern Protestant Gnosticism as a whole. By examining the Jehovah's Witnesses, we can gain a more nuanced understanding of how their beliefs and attitudes exemplify the concept.

Let me clarify that I'm not specifically targeting the Jehovah's Witnesses; I'm using them as a stark example of an advanced malignant condition that's easy to recognize in order to help you spot similar but less severe manifestations of the same condition in your own church. This approach is something we often do in our daily lives. For instance, if someone is concerned about a peculiar mole on their skin, they might search for images of advanced melanoma to see if there are any minor similarities. It's a part of human nature to have difficulty recognizing very personal issues, especially when they hit too close to home, while easily spotting similar issues in others. As the saying goes, "Our own sins never look as ugly as when someone else is wearing them."

With that graphic picture in front of you, I can begin to fill in my earlier outward characteristics more clearly and understandably.

1. MODERN GNOSTICS USE THE BIBLE

The Jehovah's Witnesses have perverted the Bible to such a degree that they were forced to create their own "New World Translation" in 1961 because none of the three thousand existing objective versions would support their twisted theologies. It must be noted that over the past two millennia, both clever and not-so-clever individuals have manipulated the words of Scripture to support their own agendas. Time and again, it's been shown that if you torture Scripture enough, you can get the words to confess to anything. Sadly, in the case of the Jehovah's Witnesses, the words were so severely tortured that there was not enough left of the victim to recognize that it had once been the living word. Thus, in 1961, after eighty years of changing the meaning of the Bible piecemeal, they were forced to start anew and create their own Bible.

Their members hold a distinctly different perspective. They believe that throughout the past two thousand years, every other church and theologian has significantly corrupted and changed the Bible. As a result, they feel that God has personally called them to restore his original message.

How could they possibly believe something that ridiculous? It all goes back to the distorted nineteenth-century religious mindset that I mentioned in the introduction. Before the Revolutionary War, there were very few "new" Christian denominations in America. However, there was a shift in the eighteenth century, and by the dawn of the nineteenth century, the floodgates had completely opened with the emergence of the Plymouth Brethren (modern mainstream dispensationalism), the Mormons, the Millerites, the ever-propagating Adventist offshoots (splintering off into groups such as the Christadelphians, the Jehovah's Witnesses, and Herbert W. Armstrong's Worldwide Church of God), and on and on down the road, splintering and dividing (and worst of all innovating) until there are a reported thirty-five thousand Protestant denominations today.

One of the fundamental tenets of the nineteenth-century restorationist groups was the Great Apostasy theory, which says that at some point, either after the death of the apostles or during the time of Constantine, the church fell completely away and ceased to exist. A belief in the Great Apostasy has been characteristic of the restorationist groups that emerged in America after the Second Great Awakening, such as the Christadelphians and the Jehovah's Witnesses.

The Jehovah's Witnesses wholeheartedly believe that the true Christian church ceased to exist and that there was no legitimate Christian church for over fifteen centuries. They assert that they alone finally restored the true apostolic church in the 1870s. Consequently, it follows that they would likewise believe that there was no genuine, untainted Bible during all that time, and they would need to restore that also.

2. MODERN GNOSTICS BELIEVE THAT THEY ALONE POSSESS BIBLICAL TRUTH

Throughout its long history, one of the most compelling aspects of Gnosticism lies in its allure for those who crave a sense of belonging to an exclusive circle of enlightened individuals. As the name Gnosticism itself declares, they are "the knowledgeable ones." There's an undeniable appeal in being part of a select group that possesses profound insight into the true nature of God—an understanding that everyone who is not part of their group, unfortunately, lacks. The members must be unassailably indoctrinated with this conviction; otherwise, their organization would not be able to send them proselytizing door to door. If they were even minimally open to dialogue, many members might be swayed by the differences of opinion they would routinely encounter. But they can't be swayed. They've been programmed to recite their spiel like robots and then just keep shuffling mindlessly along.

They are rigidly steadfast in their beliefs, confident that they are the chosen few, the enlightened ones. Most crucially, they believe they alone hold both the true knowledge and the only blueprint for salvation. Everyone who opens the door to them will either sign up or display their ignorance by rejecting the one truth. They see only those two options with anyone they talk to. It is they and their group who possess advanced spiritual knowledge, while all others are spiritually blind and deceived.

They perfectly embody what the brilliant church historian Diarmaid MacCulloch says: "One of the most unattractive features of any religious system is its insistence that it alone represents the only true or authentic [face of Christianity]. This common human pathology is based in pride."[1]

Building on that idea, A. W. Tozer insightfully proposes that the sin of pride fundamentally arises from a lack of self-awareness, which leads to an oblivious kind of self-righteous arrogance: "[The true] Christian is one who knows himself best. And the one who knows himself [best, knows that he] deserves [damnation]. The man who knows himself least is likely to have a cheerful, if groundless, confidence in his own moral worth because his concepts are only quasi-Christian."[2]

If you find that their attitudes resemble those of the Pharisees, then you're likely not far from the truth. Decades ago, a radio pastor articulated

---

1. MacCulloch, *All Things Made New*, ch. 3, 27:00.
2. Tozer, *Radical Cross*, 180.

a thought so exquisitely that it has stuck with me ever since: "The Pharisees developed a great sense of self-righteousness and spiritual pride. In their own eyes, they were the spiritual elite looking down on all the common sinners. We should all be aware of self-righteousness and how easily it attaches itself to us. Our perverse nature desires to have people think that we are extremely holy people, ultra-righteous, that we really walk close to God, that we are something special, something holy, something above the normal."[3]

Since this is how they view themselves, it's clear why they feel irked by your ingratitude in rejecting their message. They are dedicating their time and energy to help you understand the only truth, hoping that you, too, can be sure of joining them in the kingdom of God. This commitment sounds truly self-sacrificing and loving. But is their motivation purely altruistic, or are their leaders engaging them in a numbers game by having them go door to door, seeking out individuals who are struggling during difficult times while simultaneously targeting those with very low self-esteem and varying levels of personal dysfunction? It's common knowledge that these types of people can be easily brainwashed and transformed into fanatics. Finally, they can discover a sense of purpose, fueling their commitment and passion.

3. THE ALLURE TO RELINQUISH UNIQUE IDENTITIES FOR A SHARED GNOSTIC IDENTITY IS CAPTIVATING

In a very short time, these types of people are easily convinced that anyone who opposes the Jehovah's Witnesses is working for Satan, and anyone who speaks against the Jehovah's Witnesses organization is speaking against God. In their minds, the Jehovah's Witnesses organization and God are synonymous. This mindset is extremely effective in the modern world. Anyone can go to the Internet and find information countering everything about their origins, predictions, fallacies, and cult dogma. But, through a psychologically perfected process of manipulation, they have been led to believe that any perspective contrary to their own is akin to pure evil. This deep-seated conviction causes them to instinctively block out differing opinions, covering their ears and retreating whenever they encounter contrary information that they deem dangerous or corrupting. Their fear

3. Noted while listening to a decades old radio broadcast, but I cannot remember the pastor who spoke them.

of this so-called "satanic" influence drives them to run away from any discourse that challenges their beliefs.

For anyone who has ever attempted to engage in conversation with one of them, you'll understand the frustration: it's as if there's an invisible barrier that prevents meaningful communication from taking place. It's virtually impregnable. Group members take great pride in being part of what they consider the one true faith. When they meet at their conventions, they don't ask how long someone has been a Jehovah's Witness; instead, they pridefully ask, "How long have you been in the truth?"

Remember that the ancient gnostic Valentinus also played on this word by calling his fabricated gospel "the Gospel of Truth." In George Orwell's novel *1984*, the "Ministry of Truth" served as a hub for propaganda, deceit, and brainwashing. The focus on claiming an exclusive "truth" as part of one's identity should likely encourage us to view the organization making this assertion with a degree of skepticism.

4. THE GNOSTIC GUARANTEE OF SALVATION IS CAPTIVATING BECAUSE ITS ASSURANCES RESONATE WITH OUR SELF-CENTEREDNESS

Members of the Jehovah's Witnesses embrace a rather curious premise: all of Christianity completely vanished following the death of the apostles, and there have been no Christians, and therefore no one has been saved, for close to two millennia. They have also chosen to believe that every theologian from the church fathers down through the many thousands of Catholic and Protestant theologians have all been either satanically inspired or simpletons. The only figure they acknowledge as a true theological giant is a man from the late nineteenth century named Charles Russell. Remarkably, by the time Russell was out of his teens, he had unapologetically plagiarized the tenets of other religions to found their organization. One might assume that such a fact would prompt them to question the validity of the salvation guarantees provided by that same organization. However, that isn't the case at all.

It is nearly impossible for someone to set aside their fundamental human reasoning and accept such ridiculous notions unless they have been completely captivated by the alluring promise of an everlasting existence with God after death. This blindness is often accompanied by the comforting assurance of unwavering loyalty from their fellow believers while they navigate life on this earth.

5. THESE GROUPS OFTEN MAKE A CONCERTED EFFORT TO DISTINGUISH THEMSELVES FROM OTHERS, SIMPLY TO CREATE A STRONGER SENSE OF IDENTITY

The Jehovah's Witnesses possess a set of beliefs that distinctly differentiates them from mainstream Christianity.[4] Central to their faith is the rejection of the Trinity—while many Christians understand God as a triune being (Father, Son, and Holy Spirit), the Jehovah's Witnesses believe in a singular God, viewing Jesus not as divine but as a created being, distinct from God the Father.

Moreover, Jehovah's Witnesses hold a unique perspective on the afterlife, as they do not subscribe to the traditional concept of hell. Instead, they advocate for annihilationism, which suggests that those who do not attain salvation will ultimately cease to exist rather than suffer eternally.

Evangelism is a cornerstone of their practice; they prioritize sharing their beliefs and spreading their message vigorously. Their methods often include door-to-door preaching and the distribution of literature, reflecting their commitment to outreach and education about their faith.

The Jehovah's Witnesses hold a distinctive belief system centered around the idea of works-based salvation. This framework suggests that individuals must actively participate in various religious activities, including preaching to others, attending regular meetings, and adhering to strict moral and ethical guidelines in order to secure God's favor. Contrary to traditional Christian beliefs, which emphasize the concept of grace as a gift from God, the Jehovah's Witnesses do not incorporate grace into their understanding of salvation.

Up to this point, one could argue that their differences may stem from a lack of thorough scholarship rather than a conscious effort to stand apart. After all, Mormons hold some beliefs that somewhat align with the ideas

---

4. Details on Jehovah's Witness beliefs throughout comes from my own extensive interaction with the Jehovah's Witnesses over the years. However, for further reading on the topic, see Martin, *Kingdom of the Cults*; Franz, *Crisis of Conscience*; and Wilson, *Shutting the Door*.

mentioned above. However, the following points cannot be viewed in the same light.

The Jehovah's Witnesses have a unique perspective on the end times, asserting that only a select group of 144,000 individuals, the anointed, will gain entry into heaven. In contrast, the remaining Jehovah's Witnesses will enjoy eternal life on "a paradise earth." This belief is deeply rooted in the book of Revelation. Interestingly, Rev 7 explicitly identifies the 144,000 as being all Jews and outlines the number from each tribe. I've even heard pastors jokingly suggest, "If you ever meet one, why not ask him which tribe he's from?"

However, the issue at hand goes beyond tribal lineage; it delves into mathematics. These elites are a self-appointed class that rely on what they claim to be a private revelation from God to affirm their status as the anointed ones. While rank-and-file members take pride in meeting these individuals during assemblies, it might surprise you that the organization does not track their numbers. The reason is simple: after nearly one hundred and fifty years, they have significantly outnumbered the 144,000.

Additionally, the Jehovah's Witnesses follow a distinctive approach to celebrations, opting out of widely recognized holidays like Christmas and Easter, as well as personal milestones such as birthdays. They believe these occasions are rooted in pagan customs that do not align with their religious beliefs. This choice often leaves them feeling isolated from the wider society, including the broader Christian community. Consequently, their practices create more group isolation and a stronger bond among their congregational family, fostering an almost militant sense of unity and mutual support among fellow believers.

The Jehovah's Witnesses deliberately refrain from using the cross as a religious symbol, believing instead that Jesus Christ was executed on a single upright stake, not a traditional cross. This distinction appears to be an effort to set themselves apart from other Christian denominations. Founded around 1870 and claiming divine guidance from Jesus Christ since 1919, it is curious that it took until 1931 for them to assert this specific view of the crucifixion. This significant shift in the 1930s seems to have been a strategic move to foster a sense of uniqueness and enlightenment among their members.

Furthermore, they assert that only Jehovah's Witnesses will not experience the torment of Armageddon, a belief they frequently emphasize in their literature and at conventions. Critics frequently highlight a distinct enthusiasm in their discussions on this topic, which can sometimes seem almost delightfully malicious, as they believe the rest of us will inevitably face the painful consequences of not heeding their warning and joining their organization.[5]

In 1945, the organization implemented its well-known ban on blood transfusions, interpreting Acts 15:20, which calls for abstaining from blood, as a mandate for this prohibition. This seems to be a deliberate misinterpretation of Scripture meant to distinguish themselves, and sadly, many Jehovah's Witnesses have lost their lives over the years when a transfusion could have saved them.

While this group holds numerous other beliefs, I believe you can grasp the main idea. It's worth noting that Jehovah's Witness members often take pride in declaring, "We are the only ones who do this, and we are the only ones who don't do that." They firmly believe these distinctions set them apart as the one true church and "God's only organization on Earth." They are firmly convinced that they alone hold the keys to the ultimate spiritual truths.

For the sake of argument, let us now envision a scenario where only a single, true church exists, representing the sole bearer of ultimate truth. In this imagined world, this singular group would hold exclusive access to divine wisdom, guiding its followers with certainty and clarity in matters of faith and morality. How would an individual go about finding this church? Would one simply sit at home and wait for a devoted member of this elusive faith to show up at your door? Probably not. Given the thousands of diverse churches scattered throughout America, the likelihood of someone from this one true church actually knocking on your door is exceedingly slim. Instead, one might consider seeking out this church more proactively.

However, that would require incredible time and an extraordinary set of unique skills. Even more dauntingly, Joshua Schooping makes the challenge of finding the one true church seem utterly impossible. He writes,

> [If there were only One True Church, then that would send] credulous inquirers and would-be defenders of the faith on a man-centered hunt to find out which "one true church" is really the "one true church," according of course, to the investigators' (gasp!) private judgment. Now, it requires a Ph.D. in church history and

---

5. As an example of this, see Scorah's account in "Leaving the Witness."

theology together with mastery of multiple languages to find [that One Church].[6]

Clearly, finding the one true church presents numerous challenges for the average person. This "credulous inquirer" must see himself as anything but naive. He would need to have an unwavering belief in the superiority of his own sense of "private judgment," convinced that his intuition alone can lead him to the truth, even without any understanding of church history, theology, or biblical languages. This "average person" would have to be filled with pride to believe all this.

And now we've stumbled on the essence of all forms of Gnosticism: pride. In their own minds and hearts, gnostics are always the proud, exceptional people who love and know the truth. Their identity is thoroughly intertwined with that exclusive circle of individuals who believe they are the only true Christians, sharing a bond forged through continual mutual affirmation.

The pride-filled Jehovah's Witnesses claim they have the only formula for achieving eternal life, which will shortly be presented in bullet point form for clarity. Before I share their list and question whether we should all believe it, I want to ask if the Jehovah's Witnesses members themselves should even believe it. The credibility of everything they have to say ultimately depends on the credibility of their founder and the origins of their organization in the 1870s.

I'll begin with a list of beliefs:

1. We believe that God, Jehovah, is the creator of all things and the Father of true believers.

2. We reject the doctrine of the Trinity. God is One.

3. We reject a literal hell and believe that those who are not part of the coming kingdom will be annihilated (annihilationism).

4. We believe that the name Holy Spirit simply refers to the power of God the Father.

5. We believe that the traditional teachings of Christendom constitute an apostasy from the true teachings of Jesus; therefore, we have rediscovered the original teachings of Jesus.

---

6. Schooping, *Disillusioned*, 40.

6. We believe that Christendom is not biblical but is based on the traditions of men.
7. We are pacifists and will not serve in any army nor participate in any war.
8. We love and respect each other supremely because we know that we are Christ's brothers and that our love for each other serves as an example to the world.
9. Our name reflects the fact that we are God's specially chosen followers.
10. We believe in the importance of biblical teaching on morality, and obedience to the commandments.
11. We believe in a daily commitment to the things of the kingdom.
12. We are a community of Bible students and are devoted to the careful study of the Bible and its true teachings.
13. We can show that our teachings come directly from the Bible.
14. We believe that a studious inquiry into the Scriptures will lead the honest, serious believer into becoming one of us.
15. We see a philosophical contradiction between God being immortal and the death of Jesus—how can God die?
16. We believe that we will live with Christ on a restored earth.
17. We have no professional clergy.
18. Those among us who do not continue to follow God's revelation to mankind will be disfellowshipped.[7]

While the above list may seem like a verbatim, word-for-word list of the beliefs of the Jehovah's Witnesses, who were founded around 1870 by Charles Russell, it is actually a verbatim, word-for-word list of the beliefs of Dr. John Thomas, who founded the Christadelphian church in 1848. Just to clarify, four years before Charles Russell was even born in 1852 and over twenty-two years before the Jehovah's Witnesses were founded in the 1870s, the above list of beliefs was in black and white in those exact words.

Founding the "one true church" by stealing the beliefs of a little-known organization that existed before you were born was undoubtedly an unusual way for Charles Russell to begin the church that calls itself "the truth."

---

7. Damick, *Orthodoxy and Heterodoxy*, 278–81. This list is a compilation from the subchapter on "Christadelphians."

FAKE SALVATION IN MODERN GNOSTIC AMERICA

Yet, that's precisely what he did. Those ideas initially came from Dr. John Thomas, who founded the Christadelphian church in 1848. He shared that list of beliefs through his widely circulated magazines and books, making them accessible to all readers, including Charles Russell, whom he knew personally. The concepts put forth by John Thomas even made their way across the Atlantic to England, where, in the late 1840s, a branch of the Christadelphians was founded.

History reveals that numerous self-important egotists exhibited these telling traits from an early age. For example, Charles Russell had dropped out of school at the age of twelve. At age thirteen, he rejected the Calvinist Presbyterianism church in which he was raised. It seems that he believed he was educated enough and had enough knowledge about deep Calvinist theology to reject it as false. It's interesting to note that Calvin himself would not have been able to write his *Institutes of the Christian Religion* at the age of thirteen. Yet, Russell believed he had the intellectual capacity to assess and evaluate the complexities of the entire Calvinist system at such a young age.

Could the foundations of the Jehovah's Witnesses organization possibly be any less credible? Absolutely. Russell's behavior progressed from plain acts of plagiarism—where he used someone else's work without giving credit—to actions that crossed a line into outright sacrilege. The entirety of the Jehovah's Witnesses organization rests on their stated belief that Jesus returned "invisibly" in 1914 and that the times of the gentiles would end in that same year.

But why stop there? They further declare that Christ personally heads the Jehovah's Witnesses organization, his "One True Church," and has been speaking through their Governing Body since Christ appointed them in 1919. Aside from their own claims, there exists no tangible evidence to support any of those lofty assertions.

Worse still, it is a documented fact that their foundational beliefs surrounding the notion of Jesus' "invisible return" in 1914, as well as the conclusion of the times of the gentiles in the same year, were initially conceived and widely circulated by prominent Adventist figures N. H. Barbour, B. W. Keith, and J. H. Paton before the founding of the Jehovah's Witnesses (notice the bottom right-hand corner of the magazine, where the Adventists declare the "'Times of the Gentiles' end in 1914").[8] This period marked a

---

8. *Herald of the Morning*, July 1878, edited by Nelson H. Barbour, via Wikipedia, "Nelson H. Barbour."

significant moment in religious thought. Interestingly, for about two years in the late 1870s, Charles Russell himself was one of the assistant editors for N. H. Barber's Adventist magazine, *Herald of the Morning*.

That brings up an intriguing question. Having already established the one true religion in the early 1870s, which means there can only be a single path, why would Russell later become the assistant editor for a magazine promoting false Adventist beliefs?

Despite the weight of the evidence to the contrary, Charles Russell and the organization fervently embraced these beliefs as if they were their own creations. It appears that Russell, along with his group that proudly refers to itself as "the truth," has developed a troubling pattern of deceit and dishonesty. Charles Russell and the Jehovah's Witnesses did not receive the "invisible presence" idea and the 1914 date for the end of the gentiles from Jesus Christ, as they claim. It's a fact that they stole those concepts from the Adventists.

That brings to mind yet another question. Why did the Adventists go through the trouble of even inventing this fiction in the first place? They took this dramatic step to preserve their credibility after a series of miscalculations by the Adventists and the Millerites regarding the anticipated return of Christ. Since 1843, these groups had repeatedly set dates that ultimately came and went, leaving their followers disheartened and questioning both their faith and their leaders. Sometime after 1874, to try and explain their latest failure, another contributor to Barbour's magazine, B. W. Keith, cleverly decided that the Adventists did have the correct date for Christ's coming in 1874. They claimed that the date was correct but that their interpretation was wrong. It was said that while they were expecting Christ's actual return, his physical presence, what had actually happened was that Christ came "invisibly," an "invisible presence."[9] Pretty clever.

While one could argue against Christ coming physically and say, "You're wrong. Christ didn't show up," no one could conclusively argue against the claim that he came invisibly. You cannot prove or disprove that conclusively. Again, this is another example of the distorted religious mindset of nineteenth-century America that I referred to in the introduction and earlier in this chapter.

Russell and the Jehovah's Witnesses recognized the brilliance of these ideas and incorporated them into their fledgling church since they had set unfulfilled dates for Christ's return themselves. By adopting these concepts, they must have aimed to solidify their church's credibility and establish a strong theological foundation that would resonate with their followers, fill them with self-righteous pride, and help the movement to grow. And it has continued to resonate with their followers to the point of blind obedience.

9. Franz, *Crisis of Conscience*, 183.

To this day, the Jehovah's Witnesses organization still relies on these blatant falsehoods to sustain its existence. If their members were to fully recognize and accept the fact that these things are not true, the entire organization would face an immediate and total collapse, crumbling under the weight of its own lies.

I know you're hoping that we have come to the end of these overly obvious theological appropriations, and in a sense, we have. In a commendable turn, Russell appears to have repented and overcome his previous habit of copying the ideas of the Christadelphians and Adventists verbatim. Rather than accepting their ideas at face value, he decided to tap into his own creative brilliance to prove or disprove their claims.

In his book *Thy Kingdom Come*, Charles Russell tied the measurements of the internal passageways of the Great Pyramid of Giza to the date of 1914. Russell wrote, "If we measure backward down the first ascending passage to its junction with the entrance passage . . . this measures 1542 inches, which corresponds to BC 1542 . . . [then the measurement to the pit, of] 3457 inches symbolizes 3457 years from the date of BC 1542. . . .Thus, the Pyramid witnesses that 1914 [date]."[10]

It would appear that Jesus Christ agreed with Charles Russell's pyramid calculations. By June 15, 1922, Jesus Christ himself had been in charge of the Jehovah's Witnesses organization for about three years. Since, according to the Watchtower organization, Jesus speaks through them, then Jesus must have confirmed Charles Russell's math when he instructed the Watchtower to write the following:

> In the passages of the Great Pyramid of Giza, the agreement of one or two measurements with present truth chronology might be accidental, but the correspondence of dozens of measurements proves that the same God designed both the pyramid and the plan—and at the same time proves the correctness of the [1914] chronology.[11]

Then, a strange thing happened six years later. The Jehovah's Witnesses organization abandoned its pyramidology in 1928 and attempted to backtrack and erase all the traces of their claim that Jesus Christ had ever told them to write this.[12] Why would they try to erase all traces of Charles

---

10. Russell, *Thy Kingdom Come*, 342.

11. Watch Tower Society, "What Is Needed"; see the section titled "Further Proof of Present-Truth Chronology."

12. See Franz, *Crisis of Conscience*, 225, 229.

Russell and the Jehovah's Witnesses organization's heavy reliance on the Great Pyramid of Giza to prove their essential 1914 date? It could be that in 1928, the leadership of the Jehovah's Witnesses organization made a truthful, practical assessment. This pyramid stuff sounds like new-age, cultic atheism, and even though they knew that Charles Russell had plagiarized all of the prominent Jehovah's Witness doctrines from various Adventist/Millerite groups, this pyramid stuff made him and the organization look like madmen. Furthermore, none of this sounds like anything that Jesus Christ would associate himself with.

Decades later, in the early 1990s, in what at first looks like a long overdue step toward transparency, the Jehovah's Witnesses organization finally acknowledged that Charles Russell had stolen the 1914 date and its meaning from the Adventists of the nineteenth century. After a century of being utterly dishonest about this, why would the Jehovah's Witnesses organization fess up to this in the 1990s? Why not just keep this lie a closely guarded secret?

Well, they tried but couldn't. They were forced to acknowledge it because a Jehovah's Witness in Sweden named Carl Olof Jonsson released the book titled *The Gentile Times Reconsidered*, in which he spelled out the truth about the 1914 date. An obituary piece written by Eric Wilson explains why the Jehovah's Witnesses organization has kept the origins of that 1914 date hidden for over one hundred years:

> I urge all Jehovah's Witnesses to examine the evidence for their foundational 1914 Presence of Christ teaching. If the year is wrong, then everything is wrong. If Christ didn't return in 1914, then he didn't appoint a Governing Body as the Faithful and Discreet Slave in 1919. That means the leadership of the Organization is bogus. They have staged a coup, a takeover. . . .
>
> The book continues to show the Governing Body's response to Carl's treatise, which escalated from demands that he keep the information to himself and "to wait on Jehovah" to threats and intimidation tactics until, finally, they arranged to have him disfellowshipped. Shunned for speaking the truth. An increasingly familiar scenario, isn't it?[13]

Mr. Jonsson chose truth and God over lies and false religion. Disfellowship resulted in the loss of all of his so-called "loving friends." However, friendship with God was more important to him than his social life.

---

13. Wilson, "Remembering Carl Olof Jonsson."

Everything he said was verifiably true! The Jehovah's Witnesses later admitted that.[14]

All of the above illustrates the astonishing power of modern Gnosticism. Only the otherworldly power of Gnosticism can explain how people can be so self-deluded, accept such beliefs, and adhere to directives that forbid them from looking these things up on the Internet or seeking any readily available independent information. Gnosticism compels them to devote their entire lives, souls, and identities to the Jehovah's Witnesses organization and voluntarily immerse themselves in the isolating mechanisms of their group echo chamber in order to remain willfully blind to conflicting opinions and truths. Metaphorically speaking, modern Gnosticism is the most powerful "drug" out there.

Given that context, I will now list the specific requirements they have established for attaining salvation. This is the information they are so eager to convey when they come knocking on people's doors. They are driven by a deep conviction that they alone hold the exclusive knowledge that leads to salvation, and they have a particular formula that outlines this distinctive path:

- Repent of sins: People must repent of their sins and call on the name of Jehovah.
- Baptism: Baptism is a vital step toward salvation (what they precisely mean is baptism into the Jehovah's Witnesses organization).
- Preaching: Preaching is a necessary work for salvation, both for oneself and for others (what they specifically mean is door-to-door proselytizing and the handing out of Jehovah's Witness literature).
- Conform to Bible standards: People must conform to the moral requirements of the Bible.
- Support God's organization: People must be members of God's organization (which means only the Jehovah's Witnesses organization) and actively support anointed Christians (those within the group who are part of the "144,000" in the book of Revelation. These "anointed ones" have self-determined and announced that they are anointed and will be in heaven. Most of the members believe that they are the non-anointed and will reign on a restored paradise earth).
- Use the name "Jehovah": People must use the divine name "Jehovah" in worship.

14. Franz, *Crisis of Conscience*, 179.

- Avoid worldly influences: People should remove themselves from the worldly influences of nonbelievers (which means that the members are required to sequester themselves within the bubble of the organization's teachings and only associate with fellow members: the Jehovah's Witnesses are their new family now and the family they grew up with is "the world").

- Adhere to modest dress and grooming: People should adhere to strict rules of modest dress and grooming.[15]

There you have it. The above is either the one definitive, trustworthy formula for guaranteed salvation or it's the latest reincarnation of the two-thousand-year-old gnostic script designed to deceive people by appealing to human religious pride.

If it's the former, then from all of human history, only a few million modern Jehovah's Witnesses will stand before God, claiming that they met the singular requirements for salvation during their lives and have diligently checked off every box along the way. As for those who are not Jehovah's Witnesses, they believe that every one of the billions of individuals who have ever lived will face annihilation.

If it's the latter, then they will join the countless gnostic groups throughout history that Jesus cautioned us against, urging us not to be deceived. Only he has the words of life. Throughout Christian history, gnostics have always presented a carefully crafted, psychologically enticing collection of flattering words. However, none of them were life-giving. Every Jehovah's Witness magazine article, biblical exposition, teaching sermon, and guiding principle for practice and discussions during assemblies were entirely focused on instilling a profound sense of assurance among the members. That was the entire agenda and the only reason for the group's existence. The message incessantly drummed into their heads and burned into their hearts was that the Jehovah's Witnesses alone possess the unique and exclusive knowledge for securing an eternal relationship with God. This continual masterful indoctrination fosters a strong communal bond, reinforcing the belief that every one of their writings came directly from God's lips to the Jehovah's Witnesses organization's pens.

---

15. For more information on these beliefs, see Watchtower Society, "What Is Needed for Salvation?"; Rhodes, "Jehovah's Witnesses"; Wikipedia, "Jehovah's Witnesses and Salvation."

Appropriately, Philip Lee also noted that "many cults have sprung up that claim special gnosis within their own membership."[16]

Adding to their Gnosticism and self-righteousness is their own unique language. All Jehovah's Witnesses wording has been carefully selected to reinforce obedience and an us-versus-them mentality. They possess a collective language that keeps them centered and focused as a group while also reinforcing their shared identity. This common language and culture enhances group cohesion, making it easier for members to relate to one another and more challenging for them to connect with outsiders. Below are a few examples from writer Sylviane Nuccio.

1. True Christians: "Any Christian that is not a Jehovah's Witness is not a true Christian, since they believe that they are the only true Christians." (This mindset promotes superiority, elitism, and gnostic pride. They feel that God has set them apart and that only Jehovah's Witnesses enjoy a genuine relationship with God.)

2. The World: "Jehovah's Witness consider themselves to be 'no part of the world.' The world is a pejorative term in the mouth of Jehovah's Witness, which is the world as we know it. The world that we all live in." (This creates a clear distinction between members and nonmembers as all others are spiritually inferior. It also reinforces their feelings of spiritual elitism, which encourages members to value only those who are receptive to Jehovah's Witness teachings and serves to distance them from those who aren't.)

3. New Light: "[This] refers to their latest . . . understanding of a certain part of the Bible that used to be understood differently." (This updates Christ's changed message directly to their Governing Body. It allows them to dismiss documented alternate teachings from the past.)

4. The Friends: "This is how Jehovah's Witnesses refer to their co-believers." (This reinforces their bond and loyalty to the group, creating a familial sense of solidarity. It forms a close-knit community of like-minded individuals. This dynamic subtly encourages members to prioritize relationships within the organization, gradually leading to the exclusion of nonmembers from their social lives. Outsiders are often viewed as spiritual and moral adversaries. Additionally, the group's prohibition against celebrating birthdays and holidays helps

---

16. Lee, *Against the Protestant Gnostics*, 113.

to further isolate members from family and friends who do not share their beliefs.)

5. The Truth: "The truth is the religion of Jehovah's Witnesses.... Many other cults call their religion 'the truth' as well." (They believe that they alone possess the secret gnostic knowledge: "the truth.")[17]

It's now time to take a step back from the close-up picture of the Jehovah's Witnesses for the moment. Since we have enough information to recognize the basic outline of Gnosticism, let's broaden our perspective and explore the surrounding landscape. Is it possible that additional churches may be visible in the background?

This brings us back to the insightful statement made by Dave Hunt and earlier points from this book: "It is folly for anyone to imagine that man can set the requirements for salvation and impose them upon God."[18]

You saw in this chapter that the most gnostic of the American Protestant denominations, the Jehovah's Witnesses organization, has "set the requirements for salvation." You examined their meticulously compiled list. You also saw that their members, the "poster children" for Gnosticism, are willing and eager participants in this "I'm saved, we're biblical," false sense of security gnostic ruse.

Without a doubt, they are wholeheartedly dedicated to their cause, eagerly anticipating the moment when they will enthusiastically demand from God the salvation they've been "promised." They are absolutely sure that God will wholeheartedly embrace the conditions they themselves have set. In their minds, it's a belief etched in stone: a certainty that feels irrevocable—a foregone conclusion that they believe to be as inevitable as the sun rising each day.

Is this prideful, gnostic attitude exclusive to the Jehovah's Witnesses, or is it a phenomenon that is pervasive throughout the broader spectrum of American Protestantism? It raises the question of whether similar feelings of superiority, pride, and hidden knowledge are common among different denominations and congregations besides them. In the upcoming chapter, we will delve deeper into that question.[19]

---

17. Quotes in this list drawn from Nuccio, "55 Loaded Language Terms."

18. Hunt, *What Love Is This?*, 205.

19. For more information about the Jehovah's Witnesses, see Carranza, "One True Church?," and "Some Timely Truth."

CHAPTER 6

IGNORING THE CONTRADICTIONS

As DETAILED IN EARLIER chapters, millions of individuals are just as certain of their eternal salvation as Jehovah's Witnesses simply because they joined a random radio or television preacher in the sinner's prayer or participated in a live event where they made a confession of faith. Are the guarantees of salvation promised by these preachers any more credible than the guarantees of salvation promised by the Jehovah's Witnesses organization? Or are they all worthless man-made guarantees devoid of any significance in the eyes of God?

On the day these churchgoers enthusiastically demand from God the salvation they've been "promised," will they have any more success imposing their "guarantee" upon God than the Jehovah's Witnesses? Is all of this, irrespective of the intensity or scale, a manifestation of gnostic pride? If that's the case, is there a test to assess if our sense of pride is similar to that demonstrated by Jehovah's Witnesses? Yes, there is:

> Something we believe to be true can actually have a contradiction when we learn new information. At that point, we find out if we are humble or proud. If we discover a contradiction in our belief, and we are humble, we change our mind about the belief. But if we choose to ignore the contradiction and choose to believe something that has been proven to be contradictory, we are *prideful*, and we damage our brains in the long run.[1]

---

1. LeMay, *Death of Christian Thought*, 70; emphasis added.

FAKE SALVATION IN MODERN GNOSTIC AMERICA

At this stage in the book, I hope that you have uncovered at least one piece of new information that will enable you to apply the aforementioned test to your own life. If you decide to take the test, I sincerely hope it uncovers a strong sense of humility within you.

Although you'd hardly know it by listening to contemporary American sermons, the New Testament is rich with teachings on essential Christian humility. For example, the parable of the publican and the Pharisee in Luke 18 is one of the more poignant humility parables:

> And he spake this parable unto certain which trusted in themselves that they were righteous, and despised others: Two men went up into the temple to pray; the one a Pharisee, and the other a publican. The Pharisee stood and prayed thus with himself: God, I thank thee that I am not as other men *are*, extortioners, unjust, adulterers, or even as this publican. I fast twice in the week, I give tithes of all that I possess. And the publican, standing afar off, would not lift up so much as *his* eyes unto heaven, but smote upon his breast, saying, God be merciful to me a sinner. (Luke 18:9–14 KJV)

Long ago, I listened to a dispensationalist pastor expound on this parable. It will be apparent that this pastor's take on this particular parable was shaped by modern thought, as classic dispensationalism argues that a substantial portion of the New Testament isn't relevant for contemporary Christians. This perspective sheds light on the motivations behind dispensational-leaning pastors and explains some of their seemingly contradictory stances and teachings in relation to the New Testament. This particular pastor laughed out loud and then proceeded to say something like,

> I find it very hard not to assume this pharisaical attitude when I look at our church. I'm very prone to say, "Lord, thank you that our church isn't like other churches. We don't beg and [hound] people for money." [I want to tell God] how wonderful we are. Because, really, in my heart, I thank God that we are not like a lot of other churches. That's just plain honest. And I think we are better. So, I have a problem with this parable.[2]

This pastor obviously failed to appreciate the fact that the very reason that Jesus spoke this parable was deeply rooted in a common human tendency: the innate pride that encourages every group to adorn themselves

---

2. I had noted these words in the margins of my Bible while listening to a decades old radio broadcast, but I cannot remember the pastor who spoke them.

in that kind of gnostic elitist attire. By selecting a Pharisee as a negative exemplification, Jesus aimed to underscore his message—he did not wish for us to become like the faction who thought they knew more about godliness than God and who ultimately demanded that Jesus be crucified.

The Jehovah's Witnesses incessantly and skillfully implant this rock-hard, arrogant mindset in their members, and it looks like this pastor and many other modern pastors are attempting to do the same. Their overflowing reservoir of pride, which is continually topped off, is precisely why Jehovah's Witnesses are immune to change or any acceptance of truth. The above is clearly an example of a modern pastor reading from the Jehovah's Witness gnostic script.

"The publican, standing afar off, would not lift up so much as his eyes unto heaven, but smote upon his breast, saying, God be merciful to me a sinner." The actions of this humble publican could not be any more diametrically opposed to modern churchgoers who stand before God and pridefully proclaim, "I'm saved."

If we were to overlay this parable with modern souls, every member of that congregation would embody the spirit of the Pharisee. They certainly would not embody the spirit or religious attitude of the publican. The purpose of Jesus' words was clearly to warn us against this pharisaical attitude, not for us to make excuses to self-righteously adopt and justify that attitude.

This humble publican was so remorseful and disgusted with himself that he would not even raise his eyes upwards. Additionally, he beat on his chest in a display of heartfelt emotional agony and begged God with all his being to be merciful to him, even though he knew he was utterly worthless.

In stark contrast, modern American gnostic leaders do not try to cultivate this deep sense of contrition and self-reflection in their followers. Both the Jehovah's Witnesses and the mainstream churches are equally guilty in this regard. This dissonance raises significant questions about their approach and the underlying truths they embrace. Something is evidently amiss in this divergence from Scripture.

The pastor then confessed that he never had a strong affinity for this specific parable, which puts him at odds with a significant teaching of Jesus. However, this viewpoint seemed not to disturb his audience; it would only pose a concern for those who had been taught to hold the words of Christ in high regard rather than overlooking much of the New Testament, as is taught in classic dispensationalism.

The pastor transitioned to another parable from Luke 18, focusing on the story of the rich young ruler. He concluded his homily with this final reflection: "I wonder if we will meet him in heaven or not?"

The word "we" was an invitation for the entire congregation to confidently ponder the deeper implications of their certain salvation. In a manner characteristic of most American sermons, the pastor conveyed a profound message to his captivated audience. He emphasized an undeniable truth: every person present within those walls is destined for heaven. As they drove home, the only unresolved issue the pastor encouraged them to ponder concerned the eternal fate of someone long dead. You will certainly all be in heaven, but will the rich young ruler be there with you?

Some might argue that the pastor's focus renders the sermon not only irrelevant but also a distortion of the original meaning intended by Scripture. Are we to believe that Jesus forcefully spoke these parables so that future generations would engage in a trivial contemplation regarding the fate of a biblical character?

For much of church history, the contemplation that religious leaders sought to instill in their congregants as they returned home was one that penetrated deeply into the individual soul: Will you yourself spend eternity in heaven or the torments of hell? This haunting question served as the cornerstone of many sermons during a time when preachers were unencumbered by the anxiety of losing their flock to congregations that might better align with the people's own interpretations of Scripture.

Pastors aimed to evoke not a sense of complacency or comfort but rather an urgent awareness about one's spiritual standing. Each sermon was a profound endeavor to resonate with souls, compelling them to reflect on their own eternal destinies long after the final amen had been spoken, leaving an indelible mark on their hearts and minds.

The pastor's conclusion of the rich young ruler parable again moved in the opposite direction of Christian humility, just like the rest of his sermon. In prior chapters, we discovered that there's no such thing as the certainty of salvation. Prior to the last day, in any system, there is always the question of whether you had non-faith, dead faith, or no faith. Then, on the final day, Jesus reveals the unsettling possibility that what we may have possessed all along was merely "demonic faith."

It just struck me that the elders of the Jehovah's Witnesses, along with the multitude of radio and television preachers, must possess the same knowledge that Jesus intends to reveal on the last day. They, too, must be

IGNORING THE CONTRADICTIONS

able to distinguish between saving faith and demonic faith. That's the only way they could possibly confirm that everyone belonging to their organization is saved. This is another parallel between the blatantly gnostic Jehovah's Witnesses and the subtly gnostic mainstream Protestants. Only gnostics believe that God will determine salvation based on who is wise enough and spiritual enough to reside within their gnostic walls and who agrees with their gnostic theology and knowledge of Scripture.

In Matt 19, a parallel passage to the one in Luke 18, the rich young ruler similarly asks Jesus, "What good things shall I do, that I may have eternal life?" (verse 16). Dietrich Bonhoeffer comments that "the young man's inquiry about eternal life is an inquiry about salvation, the only ultimate serious question in the world."[3]

By looking around, you would hardly know that it's also the only serious question in each of our individual lives. Amidst the myriad distractions and time-wasting, banal activities we devote ourselves to, the undeniable truth remains: the only enduring outcome of anything and everything we do on this earth is the treasure we are accumulating, whether in the eternal tranquility of heaven or the torment of hell. Make no mistake about it: with each passing day, we are consciously or unconsciously investing in one destination or the other.

Alarmingly, most people, by default, are leaning toward the latter. If you take a moment to observe the world around you, it seems as though many are blissfully unaware of the critical importance of dedicating the comparative few seconds of life to prioritizing their place of residence for the upcoming trillions upon trillions of years in eternity. As a different radio pastor flippantly asked, "Where will you spend eternity? Smoking or nonsmoking?"

The Old Testament repeatedly illustrates the deep-seated human yearning to straddle two worlds: the immediate pleasures of this life and the promise of eternity. Yet, throughout its pages, God made it abundantly clear that choosing both paths is simply not an option. In today's modern, post-Christian society, however, this dichotomy is not only accepted but often celebrated, as if living a dual existence between the secular and the sacred is perfectly normal.

The entire dispensational, modern Protestant gnostic view can cause many people to miss out on critical biblical teachings, including the profound message of Matt 10:39. In that verse, Jesus delivered a powerful

---

3. Bonhoeffer, *Cost of Discipleship*, 71.

statement: "He that findeth his life shall lose it: and he that loseth his life for my sake shall find it" (Matt 10:39 KJV). Those words are crystal clear, except when filtered through the clogged gravel of contemporary American casual Christianity.

The Reformation emerged as a powerful movement emphasizing the concept of the perspicuity of Scripture, which proposed that the Bible's core message was clear and accessible, allowing individuals to interpret and understand its teachings directly and literally. Reformers, including Luther and his followers, criticized the Catholic Church for what they regarded as unnecessary and convoluted doctrines that obscured the true message of Christianity. In places like Calvin's Geneva, where the church wielded absolute power over daily life, attendance at services was not just encouraged but mandated.[4] Under this system, even the most challenging or severe passages of Scripture were accepted without question by the populace. Those who dared to challenge the theological interpretations imposed by Calvin—such as Michael Servetus and others—faced dire consequences, demonstrating the harsh reality of dissent in a tightly controlled religious environment.

Servetus must have believed that by taunting Calvin through his persistent letters, he was engaging in an intellectually stimulating game of doctrinal chess. His passion for this contest was so intense that he even ventured into the city of Geneva while cloaked in disguise.[5] This precaution underscored his acute awareness of the potential dangers awaiting him. It's possible that he thought he could provoke Calvin and then be treated as he had been treated by the Catholic French Inquisition, which had condemned him to death for his heretical writings without ever following through on their threats. On the other hand, Servetus might have believed that martyrdom would inspire other dissenters, as indeed it did.

When Servetus's disguise was uncovered in church, he quickly realized that Calvin was not someone to be taken lightly. Instead of a swift dismissal, he faced intense scrutiny and harsh judgment. Calvin's unwavering resolve to uphold his beliefs resulted in Servetus becoming a stark emblem of intolerance in Geneva. Servetus was denied the option of a relatively painless beheading and instead burned at the stake with his heretical books chained around his neck. This cruel spectacle served as a chilling reminder

---

4. Beautiful Feet, "1541 John Calvin."
5. Bredenhof, "John Calvin."

to the townsfolk of the dire consequences that awaited those who dared to challenge Calvin's interpretation of Scripture.

Calvin's authority to dictate what he believed the Bible required of Christians was a prerequisite for church unity and biblical conformity. At least in Geneva, Calvin replaced the powerful authority of the Catholic Church with his own authority, which left the congregation subject to competent, firm biblical exegesis. The dictatorial theocracy he established is evidenced by the fact that many referred to him as the "pope of Geneva."

What happens without that authority and without the leader having the power over life and death? Leo Damrosch, in his Great Course on the book *The Decline and Fall of the Roman Empire* by Edward Gibbon, made this accurate observation:

> The Reformation proves that Christianity is inherently centrifugal unless a powerful authority prevents it from splitting into fragments.[6]

Author Andrew Damick makes the same point using simpler language:

> Almost as soon as it had begun, the Protestant Reformation began to divide into factions, all with differences on major issues of theology.[7]

In the early days of the Reformation, certain state churches held significant power and used force to enforce theological conformity, allowing little space for opposing opinions. In Geneva, John Calvin held a dominant position, shaping the city's religious life with an iron grip. Innovators and free thinkers who dared to question or challenge his stringent doctrines faced dire consequences, as the oppressive environment meant that imprisonment, torture, and even a sentence of death were harsh realities for those who opposed him.

Nevertheless, many historians now reflect on the profound impact of the Reformation, observing that it marked a pivotal moment in which individuals were granted the freedom to form their own beliefs. This shift in theological perspective established a clear connection to the modern liberal religious toleration we see today. We can easily understand the far-reaching implications of the pivotal events that took place in the early sixteenth century without delving too extensively into the immediate consequences of Luther's actions. Just seven short years after Martin Luther courageously

---

6. Damrosch, "Breakup of the Empire," 27:40.
7. Damick, *Orthodoxy and Heterodoxy*, 129.

nailed his Ninety-Five Theses to the church door in Wittenberg in 1517, a pivotal moment in European history began to take shape. The German Peasants' War of 1524–1525, a tumult of anger and rebellion, was primarily sparked by the freethinking ideas of a theologian who would come to be known as history's "first communist."[8]

This figure, Thomas Müntzer, had interacted with Luther before the posting of the theses, yet he found greater inspiration in the teachings of the educated German humanists than in Luther. Müntzer emerged as one of the first of the radical reformers, a group that vehemently rejected the rigid traditional doctrines upheld by the magisterial reformers. His fervent convictions played a crucial role in sparking a transformative movement that boldly questioned the very bedrock of societal norms and religious doctrines. This upheaval was a cautionary tale for future Christians, illustrating how swiftly innovative interpretations can gain traction and turn into violent, catastrophic events.

At the heart of this turmoil were the uprisings that echoed the early tremors of the Protestant Reformation.[9] Frustrated and oppressed, the peasants rose against their tyrannical landlords and nobles, passionately demanding improved living conditions and the freedom to dictate their own lives. Their rebellion, however, was met with a merciless response; the aristocracy unleashed its professional soldiers upon them, resulting in a brutal crackdown that led to the deaths of thousands of defiant peasants.

In the wake of this tragic violence, Martin Luther penned his controversial work, *Against the Murderous, Thieving Hordes of Peasants*. This book conveyed his righteous indignation toward the rebellious peasants. It also served as a sharp rebuttal to those who sought to blame him for the uprising, framing it as a profound warning about the dangers of unchecked theological appropriation and the dire consequences of rebellion.

Unchecked theological appropriation and the freedom of individuals to cultivate their own religious beliefs stand out today as significant factors contributing to the staggering number of Protestant churches, all asserting their authority to grant guaranteed salvation to their followers based on their own interpretations of selective biblical verses. Observations made in the previous chapter showcase how members of the Jehovah's Witness community, fully persuaded by their leaders, hold an unshakable belief that

---

8. Farrell, "Thomas Müntzer."
9. Roper, "German Peasants' War."

they alone will be granted access to the heavenly kingdom. At the same time, everyone outside their ranks faces inevitable condemnation.

This false sense of security is not an isolated phenomenon; it extends across various groups whose leaders provide similar baseless reassurances. However, we rarely take a moment to consider the possibility that we may be ensnared in a contemporary religious landscape where the true power lies with the congregation. In this dynamic, we, as members, exert a veiled but undeniable influence over our pastors, subtly demanding that they tailor their messages to suit our preferences and expectations. This unwritten contract transforms the traditional roles within the church, leading to a disconcerting atmosphere where the followers may ultimately dictate the spiritual narrative.

Since we are being told what we demand to hear, why would we choose to believe it? Could it be that God holds little significance in our lives? Is it possible that we prioritize feeling reassured about our spiritual state, only to liberate ourselves to indulge in the perks of modern affluence—our desires, culinary delights, entertainment, and the myriad comforts that come with a high standard of living? Are we so eager to accept these patently absurd and easily debunked guarantees of salvation because, at the core, our focus is firmly fixed on ourselves, with God merely occupying the fringes of our existence?

This self-centric religious attitude has been insidiously disseminated throughout American society for an extended period. Perhaps we have unknowingly allowed ourselves to succumb to this relentless barrage of influences as well. In his book *America Alone*, Mark Steyn states,

> Muslims [will not reform]. They have the advantage of knowing (unlike Luther and Calvin) where reform in Europe ultimately led: the banishment of God to the margins of society.[10]

Phillip Cary elaborates on that idea in a detailed and expansive manner, exploring its implications with revealing insight:

> Modernity is in part a product of the Protestant Reformation, which broke up the unity of medieval Catholicism and gave us these competing churches. That tended to foster a kind of secularism.
>
> Modernity arises in part from the Protestant Reformation but also shapes Protestant theology. The variety of churches that arose undermined the authority of the state churches with demands for

10. Steyn, *America Alone*, 90.

> religious liberty. The turn toward experience and certainty became a characteristic quest of modernity.
>
> This demand for certainty was meant to be a comfort. You are not allowed to doubt that God loves you, that Christ is your Savior, [and] that the Holy Spirit is given to you. [Protestant] assurance of salvation is based not just on God's word but on the inner evidence of grace in the heart and the inner testimony of the Holy Spirit. Thus, the requirement of reflective faith (believing that you believe) is a key assumption behind the Protestant turn to experience.[11]

The gradual forcing of God toward the fringes of society unfolded as a slow and measurable process, primarily driven by the rising tide of secularism that has emerged from the competition among various churches. This phenomenon can be traced back to the beginnings of Modernism, where liberal theological approaches fostered a sense of democracy within religious belief systems. In this environment, followers began to wield an increasing amount of power over doctrine. This shift proved to be highly detrimental in the wake of the Enlightenment and the ascendance of Deism.

At the same time, a burgeoning movement emerged, characterized by a positive and affirming interpretation of the gospel. This new approach focused on comfort and reassurance, transforming what Jesus described as the narrow road into something far more expansive and inviting—a sprawling sixteen-lane highway filled with endless megachurches. The original depth and challenge of the faith became obscured as the masses sought a more accommodating path, ultimately reshaping the landscape of spiritual life in ways that diverged sharply from traditional teachings.

A fascinating phenomenon has emerged in a landscape teeming with thousands of competing churches, each presenting its own unique interpretation of the gospel. Parishioners find themselves engaged in a complex evaluation process, sifting through the varied doctrines and teachings of these divergent congregations. They assess the validity of each church's theology, often measuring it against their personal beliefs and interpretations.

Once they settle on a church, their commitment remains fragile and conditional. They stay only as long as the church provides an engaging experience that offers theological simplicity rather than challenge, is politically correct and broadly welcoming, fosters a socially enjoyable atmosphere, and guarantees eternal salvation. The moment a church fails to meet these

---

11. Cary, *History of Christian Theology*, 91.

diverse and evolving expectations, individuals make swift decisions to leave, often seeking out the next congregation that aligns more closely with their own views. This ongoing quest reflects a dynamic search for a version of Jesus who thinks just like them rather than a people set apart who think just like him.

This situation drastically eroded the pastor's authority, revealing how heavily his leadership relied on the judgment and opinions of the parishioners. As Dietrich Bonhoeffer insightfully noted, this dynamic set the stage for a metaphorical Christian fire sale, where the concept of grace becomes increasingly devalued and sold at cheaper and cheaper prices. I once heard a pastor creatively term this phenomenon "Burger King Christianity," humorously suggesting that churches allow congregants to "Have it your way." Albert Schweitzer, the renowned theologian, poignantly observed that people often sought "a Jesus of their own making,"[12] indicating the deep-seated tendency toward personal preference in faith.

In a previous chapter, Philip Lee articulated that "the central, unique feature of American Christianity [is] that individuals not only do choose Jesus, but choose him on their own terms."[13] This notion highlights the individualistic nature of faith in America, where personal selection overshadows doctrinal adherence. Some pastors have derisively labeled this trend as "Christianity Lite," insinuating that the watered-down, simplistic sermons are merely "Sermonettes for Christianettes"—tailored for a less demanding audience. Others have voiced their concerns about what they refer to as the "Happy-clappy church," calling these assemblies "entertainment centers masquerading as churches," which implies a disconnection from traditional worship and a shift towards a more superficial experience. The overarching idea is clear: a troubling shift in how Christianity is practiced, marked by personal preference over theological depth.

All of the above speaks of a recurring theme that seems to encapsulate the essence of American Christianity. It can likely be distilled into a succinct phrase I once encountered: "We worship our work; work at our play; and play at our worship." This saying reflects a deep irony in how priorities are often skewed, revealing a culture that places immense value on labor

---

12. Eyeons, "Retreat and Restructuring," 31. Eyeons here is discussing Schweitzer's *The Quest of the Historical Jesus*.

13. Lee, *Against the Protestant Gnostics*, 41.

and leisure while relegating spiritual engagement to a mere afterthought or "to the margins of society," as Steyn said.[14]

I mentioned the Enlightenment and Deism, which will be covered in a later chapter. Both are often described as forms of secular Protestantism, rooted in human logic and reason, a fundamentally flawed proposition. As author Devon Rose said, "Reason is a prostitute because Christian, Jewish, and Muslim theologians [as well as secular religious opponents] all equally employ her to prove their case."[15]

Many of the philosophers may have been the prostitute's best customers, as they employed her both figuratively and literally. On the figurative side, their rise to prominence had an ironic trajectory. Many of these scholars, adept in the art of persuasion and argumentation, honed their skills under the rigorous education provided by the Jesuits, renowned for their intellectual discipline.[16] Armed with both eloquence and keen insight, they skillfully wielded the Protestant critiques against Catholicism as weapons to challenge the very foundations of Christianity itself. In the eighteenth century, this intellectual revolution gave rise to Deism—a tempered, rational interpretation of Christianity that gained significant traction in England. As this movement crossed the Atlantic, it brought Unitarianism to America, profoundly reshaping religious thought and practice.

It is not merely by chance that the Unitarians dismissed the illogical concept of the Trinity and the troubling notion of hell. Furthermore, it is noteworthy that a number of American religious movements that emerged in the nineteenth century also shared this critical stance against such conventional beliefs. The Mormons, Jehovah's Witnesses, and the original Adventist groups are three such religions to embrace these concepts. None of these groups recognize that their noble-sounding "restored Christianity" is, in fact, just another version of the various generic, synthetic forms of Deism. Part of the door-to-door spiel of the Jehovah's Witnesses is finding common ground with the biblically illiterate by encouraging them to consider how illogical the concept of the Trinity is and how unreasonable the concept of eternal hell seems when considering the nature of a loving God.

Speaking of hell, the Jehovah's Witnesses teach that there is no hell and that the wicked are annihilated. Modern dispensationalists and most modern American preachers teach that there is a hell, yet simultaneously

---

14. Steyn, *America Alone*, 90.
15. Rose, *Protestant's Dilemma*, 167.
16. Gay, *Enlightenment*, 24, 55, 64.

reassure their followers that this terrifying fate does not apply to them personally. When examining the psychological impact of both these teachings, one finds little difference between the two.

With the Jehovah's Witnesses, the underlying subliminal message downplays the dire warnings Jesus offered about being led astray, suggesting instead that the fear of such outcomes is exaggerated. In reality, they suggest that if one's theological understanding is flawed, the most severe consequence one might face is annihilation—a concept that is hardly alarming. Such teachings ultimately downplay the urgency of spiritual vigilance, offering a troubling sense of security in the face of existential risks.

With dispensational and modern American preaching, the subliminal message is eerily similar. You are assured that the concept of hell does not pertain to you, allowing you to find comfort in the notion that all of Jesus' fervent admonitions about eternal damnation are not directed at you personally. You can place your trust in the pastor without hesitation.

You have the wisdom to be wary when it comes to significant financial matters—like if someone were to approach you with a tempting offer to sell the Brooklyn Bridge at an unbelievably low price. In such a case, you would immediately see the absurdity of the claim, recognizing that the bridge isn't theirs to sell. Yet, strangely enough, we tend to ignore this kind of common sense when entering a church.

After all, we're not talking about something important, like your money; instead, the pastor is offering you peace of mind on a matter that you purposely downplay yourself. For just a modest donation, we'll guarantee your salvation. It even rhymes—as a good advertising jingle should—and you can see how this trade benefits both. You simply need to set aside any doubts stemming from the fact that he, like the Brooklyn Bridge guy, does not own heaven, although playfully pretending that he does is convenient for both of us. Let that knowledge fade into the background as we engage in this comforting and symbiotic agreement, and leave it at that.

In today's society, discussions about the concept of hell have become increasingly rare, almost shrouded in silence. Given this lack of conversation and that it's undoubtedly related to the awarding of fake salvation, it seems fitting to take a quick look at that subject.

The adage "Life is short and eternity is long" used to resonate deeply in the not-so-distant past. In eras when the specter of mortality loomed large—when childhood often ended far too soon, and many adults faced their final days in their early thirties—people possessed a sobering understanding of life's brevity that sometimes escapes us today in America.

In our fast-paced lives, we often overlook the other side of the coin when talking about salvation by completely dismissing the stark reality of hell. We seldom take the time to pause and genuinely reflect on what "hell" truly signifies. As Steve Gregg expertly argues in his book *All You Want to Know About Hell*, the stakes surrounding the idea of hell are immensely high, and "when it comes to hell, we can't afford to be wrong."[17]

Surprisingly, many of us do not live our lives with a sense of urgency regarding this reality; as Gregg notes, "No one lives as if he really believes that all around him millions of people are heading for eternal hell."[18] This lack of seriousness is troubling, as we often regard hell as a distant consequence that befalls those who are not part of our specific church community. Such a mindset is not only gnostic but also perilous, leading us to dismiss the gravity of our own potential fate.

Gregg's caution is notable; he suggests it's "safest to maintain the most pessimistic position, the worst-case scenario."[19] Embracing this perspective may encourage us to confront the uncomfortable truths about our beliefs and the eternal destinies of those around us, fostering a deeper understanding of both salvation and hell.

Yes, it is safest to maintain the most pessimistic position. If we ever endeavor to read our Bible seriously rather than superficially, we will find that certain passages are frighteningly chilling. One of the most notable is Matt 10:28: "Do not fear those who kill the body and cannot kill the soul. Rather fear him who can destroy both soul and body in hell."

Jesus is speaking directly to the early Christian martyrs who, in a short time, would be crucified, covered with tar and set on fire to light royal parties, tortured, murdered in the arena, torn apart by wild animals, encased in brass bulls and slowly cooked to death as people amusingly listened to their death throes emanating from the bull's open nostrils, and many more unthinkable tortures.

He instructs the martyrs to prepare themselves to withstand every conceivable form of torture that ancient society could devise. He urges them not to "shrink back" (Heb 10:39) in those crucial final moments, lest they find themselves consigned to hell. More importantly, he implores

17. Gregg, *All You Want to Know*, 142.
18. Gregg, *All You Want to Know*, 34.
19. Gregg, *All You Want to Know*, 40.

IGNORING THE CONTRADICTIONS

modern people to think about the grim reality of every torment inflicted upon prisoners of war or the chilling acts carried out by ruthless dictators, drug lords, and historical tyrants like Stalin, Hitler, and Saddam Hussein. The sheer brutality of these acts often leaves us in denial, unwilling to even hear—or imagine—the details of the horrific devices and methods employed by the most barbaric individuals throughout history. I remember attending an exhibition in Balboa Park, San Diego, that showcased torture devices from the Spanish Inquisition. The haunting displays kept me awake for a month as the images lingered in my thoughts, reminding me of the depths of human cruelty.

Jesus is telling us that even those horrors are nothing compared to hell. Those tortures will all end with your death, even if it takes a week or two, as is reportedly the case with being flayed alive and other tortures. The torture of hell will never end, so Jesus is making the point that nothing you endure in this life is even remotely comparable to the agony of hell.

Many have noted that the excruciating torment of hell is beyond any present comprehension, largely because we lack a frame of reference for a scenario in this life where there exists an absolute void of hope and no possibility of change. Even in our most harrowing moments, we cling to the notion that death may bring an end to our suffering, offering a release. In contrast, hell embodies a relentless state of despair, devoid of any glimmer of hope for alteration in one's fate. This perpetual stagnation, some argue, is among the most agonizing aspects of the hellish experience, as it represents a condition utterly foreign to us. The idea of enduring unending agony without the prospect of relief or change is a profound horror that should challenge our understanding of what's at stake in this life.

However, most of us remain entirely unconcerned. The guy selling the religious version of the Brooklyn Bridge gave his personal assurance. This perspective isn't merely a cynical jab; even those who identify as secular often find humor in the antics of late-night televangelists, drawing a notable comparison between these figures and used-car salesmen. The televangelists' over-the-top promises and ostentatious presentations evoke a sense of skepticism and amusement. Their theatrical pitches, laden with hyperbole, mirror the bold claims and flashy approaches of those peddling secondhand cars, making it easy for onlookers to see the similarities. Interestingly, even when similar words and assurances come from pastors we hold in high esteem, we seem unable—or perhaps unwilling—to recognize any similarities between the two.

You might also find it challenging to recognize some of the fundamental Bible truths that the individuals I've cited throughout this book have articulated. This difficulty likely stems from the fact that much of what you've encountered about Christianity has been penned relatively recently—mainly within the last two hundred years and more specifically, in the last sixty.

As we have traversed further down the path of gnostic Christianity, there have been only a handful of voices that have dared to dissent from contemporary thought. One of the most notable figures in this regard, who consistently conveyed accurate biblical truths in the post–World War II era, was A. W. Tozer. Though he passed away in 1963, even then, Tozer was an unwelcome speaker, as his incisive critiques of the emerging mindset of easy-believism were often met with resistance. In a considerable understatement, it was noted that "he was usually out of step with many of the people in the religious parade."[20]

Tozer stood out in an era when churchgoers donned their "Sunday best" attire—an expression that evokes a time when congregants approached worship with a spirit of solemnity and sincerity. This was long before the advent of the more casual, vaudeville-inspired style of entertaining worship. A small sampling of his words will shed light on why he stood out:

> If the rich man with difficulty enters the kingdom of God, then it would be logical to conclude that a society having the highest percentage of well-to-do persons in it would have the lowest percentage of Christians, all things else being equal. If the "deceitfulness of riches" chokes the word and makes it unfruitful, then this would be the day of near fruitless preaching, at least in the opulent West.[21]

> It is a grave error for us evangelicals to assume that the children of God are all in our communion and that all who are not associated with us are ipso facto enemies of the Lord. The Pharisees made that mistake and crucified Christ as a consequence.[22]

> It is scarcely possible in most places to get anyone to attend [church] where the only attraction is God. One can only conclude that God's professed children are bored with him.[23]

---

20. Tozer, *Best of A. W. Tozer*, 7.
21. Tozer, *Man*, 85.
22. Tozer, *Man*, 7.
23. Tozer, *Man*, 74–75.

IGNORING THE CONTRADICTIONS

For millions of Christians, God is no more real than he is to the non-Christian.[24]

It is hardly a matter of wonder that the country that gave the world instant tea and instant coffee should be the one to give it instant Christianity.[25]

Instant Christianity is 20th-century orthodoxy.[26]

The [true] Christian finds that after his conversion, he is not at home here.[27]

The most godly Christian is the one who knows himself best, and [the] one who knows himself [is fully aware] that he deserves hell.[28]

Do not allow yourself to be patted to sleep in a comfortable church.[29]

The sense of companionship which [you] mistakenly attribute to the presence of Christ may and probably does arise from the presence of friendly people.[30]

Always remember: You cannot carry a cross in company.[31]

We may need to break [from] the lifeless gospel churches [in] protest [of] the frivolous character of much that passes for Christianity.[32]

One cannot long read the Scriptures sympathetically without noticing the radical disparity between the outlook of the men of the Bible and that of modern men. We are today suffering from a secularized mentality.[33]

And finally,

The old Cross slew men; the new cross entertains them. The old Cross condemned; the new cross amuses. The old Cross destroyed

---

24. Tozer, *Pursuit of God*, 50.
25. Tozer, *Best of A. W. Tozer*, 103.
26. Tozer, *Best of A. W. Tozer*, 105.
27. Tozer, *Radical Cross*, 138.
28. Tozer, *Radical Cross*, 180.
29. Tozer, *Radical Cross*, 90.
30. Tozer, *Radical Cross*, 90.
31. Tozer, *Radical Cross*, 36.
32. Tozer, *Knowledge of the Holy*, 116.
33. Tozer, *Knowledge of the Holy*, 66.

confidence in the flesh; the new cross encourages it. The old Cross brought tears and blood; the new cross brings laughter.[34]

Although A. W. Tozer's words are as accurate and relevant as if they had been written this morning, most of them were penned in the 1950s. Even then, the handwriting was on the wall regarding the gnostic direction that the fake salvation American church would take, and Tozer just read it and penetratingly commented on it.

The concept of "the new cross" was just beginning to take root when Tozer penned those stern remarks. However, this troubling recent decline in religious faith was merely the culmination of a prolonged and tumultuous journey—a dramatic narrative spanning approximately seven hundred years, fraught with monumental events and profound societal shifts. This intricate history, filled with catastrophe and transformation, will be explored in greater detail in the following chapter.

---

34. Tozer, *Radical Cross*, 174–75.

CHAPTER 7

HOW DID WE GET HERE?

IN CHAPTER 2, I referenced Hugh McLeod's insightful words: "The 1960s [saw] a rupture as profound as that brought about by the Reformation. The seventeenth, eighteenth, and nineteenth centuries had seen the gradual introduction of religious toleration and a trend toward greater religious pluralism." By "the 1970s, Western societies were pluralist, post-Christian, or secular." It was "a culmination of a long-term process of secularization, going back to the Renaissance and the Reformation; a progressive marginalization of [the Christian] religion."[1]

When McLeod refers to the term "Renaissance," he undoubtedly encompasses all those pivotal occurrences leading up to this transformative period. This approach mirrors his use of the term "Reformation," which encapsulates a wide array of issues, including the various abuses within the Catholic Church, the practice of selling indulgences, Martin Luther's bold challenge to ecclesiastical authority, and the ripple effects that followed. Similarly, the word "Renaissance" evokes an expansive chronicle that embodies an era shaped by the intense and complex historical backdrop that preceded it, emphasizing how these monumental changes were born from a confluence of factors that defined the time.

This chapter traverses a significant timeline, spanning roughly 678 years from around 1347 to the present day. It outlines the key events that paved the way for the gradual shift toward secularism and the emergence of modern gnostic Christianity. It's clear that one could quickly fill countless volumes with the stories, events, and transformations that have occurred

1. McLeod, *Religious Crisis of the 1960s*, 1, 2, 8.

during such a lengthy time frame. While this single chapter can only provide a brief overview, it aims to serve as a foundational blueprint of this fascinating history, with the primary focus being on the profound changes in the attitudes of Christian people in response to the changes in the world.

While that specific focus skips over the entire substantive era between the crucifixion and 1347, it may be beneficial to quickly note a pivotal period in the eleventh century that bears relevance to the theme of this book and exemplifies a religious abuse that set the stage for the codifying of these types of abuses. After centuries of friction, a complete split emerged in 1054 between the Eastern Greek Orthodox Church and the Western Roman Catholic Church. This critical moment was driven not just by theological disputes but was significantly impacted by the individual personalities and egos involved, which overshadowed the essential issues at hand. One of the many impacts of that split was that the Eastern church and the Western church freed themselves from each other's oversight.

A few decades later, an unrestrained Pope Urban II started to advocate for the First Crusade (1096–1099). He promised forgiveness and absolution for all past sins to those who would fight to reclaim the holy land from Muslims and liberate the Eastern churches. The pope was promising salvation to those who acknowledged his authority to make such an offer, urging them to risk their lives in service of his mission. Many people placed their trust in the pope and believed wholeheartedly in the authenticity of his promise, and thousands of them enlisted to head east and fight.

Pope Urban's call to arms for the First Crusade was imbued with promises of extraordinary spiritual rewards. However, his offer was not solely reserved for those who would take up the sword and march toward battle; even those who could not physically join the fight had the opportunity to secure their place in heaven. By paying a specified sum, they, too, could reap the divine benefits, effectively putting salvation within reach for anyone willing to invest in it.

This practice inevitably evolved into the controversial practice of monetary indulgences, driven by a later theology that sought to justify such transactions. Central to this concept was the notion of a "Treasury of Merit," likened to a spiritual bank account. This treasury was said to be replenished by the virtuous deeds of Jesus Christ, the Virgin Mary, and a multitude of saints. The merits accumulated in this celestial storehouse were then made available to the faithful, allowing them to purchase grace and absolution for a price, thereby intertwining commerce with the core tenets of salvation, playing a crucial role in generating substantial income for the medieval church.

Many have labeled the sale of indulgences as one of the most cunning money-making schemes in church history, which was enlarged through the propagation of the doctrine of purgatory. People could purchase time off from purgatory for themselves or deceased loved ones. Critics often mocked this practice, pointing out that Catholics were essentially paying to release themselves or their relatives from a place that didn't exist. This practice of exchanging money for grace became a significant point of conflict between Martin Luther and the Catholic Church, igniting heated debates and frustrations that ultimately fueled the flames of the Reformation.

To contemporary people, this obviously manipulative charade is remarkably transparent. Pope Urban lacked authority over God, and regardless of how he attempted to support his offer with scriptural-sounding justifications, he did not own heaven and had no legitimate right to guarantee salvation to anyone. "It [was] folly [for the pope and the Crusaders] to imagine that man can set the requirements for salvation and impose them upon God."[2]

One can't help but wonder if, in the future, people will look back on this easy-believism era in America and wonder how churchgoers could have been so willingly gullible. Will they easily recognize what many fail to see today: that, like the pope, our modern religious leaders, from those in the Jehovah's Witnesses down through and including the thousands upon thousands of leaders of every other Protestant denomination, do not have authority over God? No matter how they may have tried to frame their offers with scriptural-sounding justifications, they, too, did not own heaven and had no legitimate right to guarantee salvation to anyone.

Now, we can delve into the pivotal year of 1347, a time that would mark the beginning of an influential, sweeping change in Christian history. The Black Death, a devastating pandemic that swept through Europe between 1347 and 1352,[3] was the monumental event that fundamentally altered the landscape of Christianity. The echoes of this tumultuous period still resonate in modern society, shaping our understanding of faith and community to this day. While this catastrophic plague decidedly wreaked havoc on the fabric of society, politics, and the economy, its most devastating and profound long-term effect was the unsettling transformation

---

2. Hunt, *What Love Is This?*, 205.
3. Mark, "Religious Responses."

in the hearts and minds of Christian devotees. For many, the devastating toll of the plague ignited a crisis of faith as individuals began to question their devotion and commitment to God in the face of such overwhelming suffering.

The calamity paved the way for the rise of humanism and the Renaissance—two movements prioritizing human experience and reason over divine authority. As the death toll climbed, a pervasive sentiment emerged: God, once seen as a protector, felt distant and uncaring; the clergy, who were expected to provide solace and guidance, seemed to offer little more than empty rituals in the face of relentless despair.

Compounding this crisis was the grim reality that the priests, entrusted with administering last rites to the dying, were themselves far more vulnerable to the plague. Their proximity to suffering and death resulted in a staggering mortality rate that far exceeded that of the general population. To the terrified, irrational Europeans, unaware of how diseases like the plague were transmitted, it seemed as though God had purposely singled out these spiritual leaders. This belief not only reinforced the idea that divine protection was lacking during this bleak period but also suggested that the church bore some responsibility for the situation.

This convergence of fear, confusion, and disillusionment reshaped Europe's spiritual environment. As the plague swept across Europe, it became increasingly evident that many began to see the church not as a bastion of faith but as an institution that had been rendered impotent in the face of human suffering. This dramatic shift in perspective laid the groundwork for a more secular viewpoint emerging in the following years, forever altering the relationship between humanity and God.

To truly understand the profound psychological impact of widespread disease, we need only reflect on the far-reaching consequences of the modern COVID-19 pandemic. It has fundamentally shaken various facets of life—economics, politics, societal unity, and, perhaps most crucially, the very attitudes of individuals worldwide. Historically, the Black Death is the most infamous plague outbreak of the medieval period. This catastrophic event unleashed an unrelenting torrent of suffering and loss, claiming millions of lives. Its enduring legacy left an indelible mark on the collective memory of humanity, echoing through the ages. The devastation it wrought remained unparalleled until the flu pandemic of 1918–1919 arrived, another unprecedented crisis that starkly illustrated the relentless impact of infectious diseases on societies throughout history.

HOW DID WE GET HERE?

It's important to consider that during the COVID-19 pandemic, the death toll was less than half a percent of Europe's total population. A little over two million people lost their lives out of a population exceeding seven hundred million.[4] This crisis occurred in a modern era where we have a clear understanding of viruses and their transmission between individuals. Additionally, we had access to vaccines, various medical treatments, and well-equipped hospitals.

In stark contrast, the fourteenth-century Black Death claimed the lives of one-half to two-thirds of the population, killing roughly fifty million people out of a population that was under one hundred million.[5] This catastrophic event struck at a time when medical knowledge was almost nonexistent, leaving people in a state of confusion and fear, completely unaware of the nature of the disease. There were no vaccines or medications available to combat the spread, resulting in widespread panic and suffering.

Joshua J. Mark examines the catastrophic events surrounding the Black Death in his article titled "Religious Responses to the Black Death," published on April 16, 2020, on the World History Encyclopedia website. He delves into the profound, long-term societal and spiritual changes that emerged in the wake of the devastating plague. By reflecting on these transformative shifts, he highlights how they have resonated throughout history and continue to shape our world today.

Below are several key takeaways from his article, followed by my commentary on each point to provide greater clarity and insight.[6]

> The recorded responses to the outbreak come from Christian and Muslim writers primarily since many works by European Jews—and many of the people themselves—were burned by Christians who blamed them for the plague.

While the plague began in Central Asia, its spread was fueled mainly by the active commerce and military movements along the Silk Road. As merchants and soldiers traveled this vast network of trade routes, they not only exchanged valuable goods and secured territorial gains but also inadvertently carried the plague with them.

---

4. Gagliardi, "Coronavirus."
5. Dattani, "Black Death."
6. The quotes in the discussion following are from Mark, "Religious Responses."

FAKE SALVATION IN MODERN GNOSTIC AMERICA

> The first recorded outbreak of bubonic plague [was] the Plague of Justinian (541–542 CE), which struck Constantinople in 541 CE and killed an estimated 50 million people....
>
> ... The disease maintained this pattern in the East, [seemingly disappearing only to resurface, until it gained] momentum ... and was raging by 1346 CE.
>
> It was around this time that the Mongol Khan Djanibek (r. 1342–1357 CE) was laying siege to the port city of Caffa (modern-day Feodosia in Crimea), which was held by the Italians of Genoa.

Mark opens his discussion with a poignant reflection on a grim, repetitive aspect of Christian history. We would probably have many more objective accounts of the plague and many other eras of history had Christians not been so eager to kill a particular group of perpetual outsiders who were always viewed with hostility and suspicion: the Jews. Many educated and articulate individuals who could have provided nuanced perspectives were tragically silenced, often at the hands of their own communities. This loss not only stunted our understanding of that horrific time but also deprived us of more diverse religious viewpoints that might have emerged from those voices. The narrative is further darkened by the unfortunate human tendency to seek scapegoats in times of crisis. Communities often succumbed to fear and paranoia, instinctively blaming the Jews in a misguided attempt to restore order. In doing so, they believed that killing these "others" would be the first crucial step toward reversing their misfortunes—an impulse that has marred the course of history time and again.

Joshua Mark then highlights the alarming reality of the earlier epidemics of plague in the Eastern regions, a grim shadow lurking in the annals of their history. Despite one of its worst outbreaks in the sixth century, the West remained largely unaffected at that time, which allows us to overlook the profound suffering it caused. The staggering toll of fifty million lives lost in the East serves as a stark reminder of the plague's ferocity; it's an incomprehensible figure when placed against the backdrop of a world population of approximately three hundred million during that time.

He next dedicates a few brief sentences to the Mongol siege of Caffa in the mid-fourteenth century and its pivotal role in unleashing the plague in Europe. Vivid and graphic tales recount the stench of decaying, putrid corpses of Mongol army plague victims being mercilessly hurled over the walls by catapults and then splattering on the defenders inside the city like rotten fruit. In a desperate bid for survival, the besieged inhabitants fled Caffa, boarding ships that would carry the devastating contagion to port cities across Europe, igniting a tragic epidemic that would alter the course of history.

> The plague raged on, and God seemed deaf to the prayers and supplications of believers. In Europe, the perceived failure of God to answer these prayers contributed to the decline of the medieval Church's power....
>
> ... The seeming ineffectuality of the Christian response to the people of the time caused many to question the vision and message of the Church and seek a different understanding of the Christian message and walk of faith. This impetus would eventually contribute to the Protestant Reformation and the change in philosophical paradigm [that] epitomizes the Renaissance.
>
> A number of Christian European writers of the time, and afterward, refer to the Black Death as "the end of the world." ... In the aftermath of the Black Death, Europe would be radically transformed in social, political, religious, philosophical, medical, and many other areas.

The next target of the people's ire was the Catholic Church. By the mid-fourteenth century, a growing awareness began to take hold among the people: the Catholic Church was experiencing a notable downturn in its influence as well as in its moral and spiritual authority. The church was growing increasingly secular, mired in corruption, and finding it hard to maintain consistency and even its traditional locale.

During the years spanning from 1309 to 1377, the papacy had shifted its seat of power from Rome to the distant city of Avignon, France, further estranging itself from the daily realities of the faithful. Discontent simmered among the laity and clergy alike, as many criticized the pervasive corruption and numerous abuses that plagued the institution. The state of the clergy was particularly troubling; a significant number of parish priests were not only illiterate but also lacked proper liturgical training, and in some cases, their conduct toward their congregations was hardly reflective of their sacred vows.

A profound sense of dread gripped the hearts of many Christians who believed they were witnessing the end of the world. In this time of terror, it seemed that God had turned a deaf ear to their fervent prayers and earnest fasting. The ghastly toll of the Black Death swept mercilessly through towns and villages, leaving a trail of despair in its wake. As the relentless disease ravaged entire communities, a wave of frustration and disillusionment surged among the faithful. Their anger toward the Catholic Church deepened as it became painfully evident that the institution was powerless and overwhelmed, unable to provide the support and solace that the people desperately needed.

The reality was grim; countless local priests succumbed to the plague, while others fled their parishes in a desperate bid for survival. This sudden loss of spiritual leadership seriously affected religious life, leaving congregations with far too few priests to uphold the traditional schedule of services and rituals that had once been a cornerstone of their spiritual community. The resulting vacuum created a sense of chaos and uncertainty, further eroding the church's authority and control over the faithful.

When Joshua Mark discusses individuals searching for "a different understanding of the Christian message and walk of faith," we are getting to the heart of the issue: the plague's long-term spiritual ramifications. Before the Black Death, the prevailing view of a Christian's role in the universe revolved around obedience; people were expected to live their lives in a manner that prioritized honoring God above all else. However, in response to the Black Death, many reacted with a sense of childlike indignation, feeling as though God had broken his end of the deal, and thus, he seemed less deserving of their unquestioning obedience and wholehearted worship. As they grappled with feelings of resentment—if not outright blame—toward God, they began to question the long-standing arrangement of their faith.

Although it would take another one hundred and seventy years before Luther's actions ignited the Protestant Reformation, the acute changes experienced by the European populace following the Black Death created a profound and rapid religious and cultural transformation long before that pivotal moment in history. It's worth reiterating that significant ideas are welcomed only when societal changes create a readiness for them, fostering an environment where new thoughts can be shared openly. During the fourteenth century, bold thinkers began to quietly question the strictly religious perspective on life, but expressing such views openly was risky, as challenging the authority of the Catholic Church could have dire consequences.

By 1347, Petrarch, widely recognized as the "Father of Humanism," was around forty-four years old, and the moment for his influence had finally arrived. He played a key role in igniting the humanist Renaissance across Europe. The populace of Europe was now ready to embrace the ideals of humanism and open to fundamentally reshaping the prevailing religious and cultural framework of the West.

The influence of humanism has been significant, especially in the context of Christianity, which has existed in its shadow since the Black Death. At its core, humanism embodies a renewed appreciation for the value and power of the individual. This movement emphasizes two key principles: individualism and secularism, both of which began to resonate among the people at the time. As society began to embrace individual thought and secular values, there was a noticeable shift away from blind obedience and unwavering devotion to God. This marked the beginning of McLeod's "progressive marginalization of [the Christian] religion."[7]

Humanism provided the foundation for much of modern Western thought. This movement emerged during a time when many individuals fleeing the East were bringing with them ancient Greek and Roman writings. Renaissance thinkers aimed to weave these classical pagan ideas into their belief systems while still holding on to their Christian roots.

With the rise of humanism, people began to shift their focus more toward this present life rather than the afterlife, which had been the norm during the Middle Ages. This attitude even extended to the lower classes, as the peasant population suddenly had the opportunity to aspire to a better life than the meager existence they had endured previously. The catastrophic loss of life had markedly diminished the workforce, leaving the once-vibrant fields dotted with empty homes and abandoned farms. Wealthy landowners, faced with a significant labor shortage, were forced to improve the living standards of the remaining workers. This shift encouraged peasants to gravitate toward areas that provided better working conditions and higher wages, empowering them to rely on their own human potential rather than depending solely on the supernatural.

What happens when both society and Christianity choose to empower the individual, merging Christ with humanist secularism? This combination leads to a situation where the genuine worship of God is placed in a secondary position to the here and now, ultimately prioritizing humanity over divinity. Over the centuries, this small seed evolved into something significant, leading to what we now identify as modern post-Christian religiosity, particularly evident in Europe.

While this overview of the years 1347 through 1352 is brief, it's essential to recognize that the religious repercussions of the Black Death played a significant role in sparking the Protestant Reformation. The catastrophic plague set off a wave of profound societal changes that laid the foundation

---

7. McLeod, *Religious Crisis of the 1960s*, 8.

for revolutionary movements within Christianity. As the disease spread relentlessly, it not only wiped out countless lives but also triggered a subversive crisis of faith among the populace. This turmoil created an environment conducive to questioning established beliefs and practices. Such a shift opened the door for new ideologies to emerge, fostering a unique atmosphere that both challenged and reshaped the religious dynamics of Europe.

In the southern regions of Europe, the humanist Renaissance blossomed through innovative perspectives in art, emphasizing the beauty and complexity of the human experience. Artists and thinkers drew inspiration from the secular themes of classical antiquity, exploring motifs of individualism and nature in their works. In contrast, Northern Europe experienced a different yet significant wave of the humanist Renaissance, which centered on a profound reevaluation of Christian themes. This intellectual movement laid the groundwork for the Protestant Reformation, prompting scholars and theologians to reexamine Scripture and religious practices.

This humanist era marked a significant transformation in how individuals interacted with various fields, including art, religion, philosophy, and science. During this period, the emphasis shifted dramatically to place humanity at the forefront of these disciplines, encouraging a renewed affirmation of human potential, creativity, and intellect. Humanity started to mold beliefs and systems around their own understanding and sense of justice and fairness, prioritizing personal experience and insight over traditional doctrines. This pivotal shift marked a celebration of man's capacity for reasoning, expression, and exploration, reshaping the cultural landscape for generations to come.

Concurrent with the humanist Renaissance, a number of other forces steadily eroded the power and influence of the Catholic Church over the next one hundred and fifty years. Among the most significant of these forces was the advent of the printing press in 1440, which revolutionized the dissemination of information, enabling new ideas to spread rapidly and widely, thus encouraging more people to question established beliefs. Additionally, incidents such as the Western Schism, a tumultuous period from 1378 to 1417 during which rival popes simultaneously claimed authority, further fueled widespread skepticism regarding the church's leadership and legitimacy. Together, the above elements laid the groundwork for ultimately reshaping the entirety of Christianity.

With that background, we can now embark on a very brief exploration of the Reformation, focusing not on its origins but rather on the trajectory it swiftly took. In the face of the numerous distortions and excesses within the Catholic Church, Martin Luther emerged with a sense of optimism, believing he could address and rectify the glaring issues from within the institution itself. By the dawn of the sixteenth century, a chorus of dissenting voices had already begun to rise, challenging the church's practices and advocating for significant reforms. Among these reformers was the intelligent, articulate, and tactful Desiderius Erasmus, whose insights and calls for change resonated deeply within the hearts and minds of many who sought a more authentic expression of faith.

Erasmus, a prominent Renaissance humanist, is often viewed as a precursor to the Protestant Reformation. However, he eventually distanced himself from Martin Luther, primarily due to disagreements over Luther's sectarian approach. Before their notable literary dispute—Erasmus wrote *On Free Will*, which Luther countered with *On the Bondage of the Will*—the Catholic Church perceived Erasmus as partly accountable for Luther's ascent. In the early stages of the Reformation, many believed that Erasmus and Luther were aligned in their efforts for reform, viewing them as collaborators in a shared cause. This initial perception was dispelled by their eventual falling out, which highlighted the deepening rifts within the movement for religious change.

Luther found himself in a situation where he had no choice but to distance himself from the church despite his longing to stay connected to it. The actions and stances taken by the pope and the church hierarchy ensured that there would be no dialogue with Luther, only increasing hostility, threats, and repression. However, the Catholic Church and Erasmus were merely the first hurdles that Luther would encounter.

In prior chapters, we examined the German Peasants' War of 1524–1525, for which Luther was blamed, and the problems caused by his former freethinking humanist associate, Thomas Müntzer, history's "first communist." We also mentioned that "Luther wrote *Against the Antinomians* to refute the erroneous teaching of the neo-Lutheran antinomian Johannes Agricola."[8] Both the peasants and those two men had taken Luther's writings in an unapproved, troublesome direction.

However, Luther's entire system had a built-in troublesome direction due to his egotistical assumption that anyone who read the Scriptures

---

8. Ligonier Editorial, "Legalism and Antinomianism?"

would interpret them as he did. He believed that the perspicuity of Scripture—its clear and obvious meaning—would be apparent to all. The inherent flaw in Luther's reasoning, as well as in the reasoning of many others, is highlighted by the fact that if the meaning of Scripture were truly obvious, we wouldn't have witnessed the rise of countless Protestant denominations.

Luther's conviction that everyone would interpret Scripture through his lens was misguided. It's evident that he fell victim to a self-imposed illusion of obviousness. His heated confrontation with Zwingli highlighted a crucial aspect of the Protestant dilemma: both men believed that their understanding of salvation was entirely dependent on the Holy Spirit, who alone provided them with the correct interpretation of Scripture.

Luther asserted that he held the ultimate truth because he interpreted the Scriptures through the Holy Spirit's guidance, which also justified his sense of security regarding his own salvation. On the other hand, Zwingli similarly claimed that he possessed the truth, having interpreted Scripture under the same divine illumination, giving him reassurance about his salvation as well. However, as mentioned in earlier chapters, this presented a significant dilemma: neither figure had clear criteria to distinguish between true certainty and false certainty, nor could they differentiate between genuine interpretation and misguided interpretation.

Thus, the Reformation had a significant vulnerability: many individuals believed they were guided by the Spirit, yet there was no established system to measure the validity of the myriad interpretations that emerged. In contrast, the Catholic Church possessed a mechanism that facilitated consensus. Regardless of whether the decisions made were ultimately right or wrong, and unfortunately, over their long history, some have been wrong, this system effectively put an end to debates, which in turn prevented the emergence of alternative Catholic churches based solely on the interpretations of an individual or a specific group. Fast forward to today: the growing number of Protestant denominations illustrates how divisions have continued, with reports of a new denomination cropping up almost every week. The theological disparities have become so pronounced that a shared definition of Protestantism across all thirty-five thousand denominations is simply that they are neither Catholic nor Greek Orthodox. Even more concerning, as this book emphasizes, is the fact that the one consistent doctrine that seems to apply to all these groups is their claim that they are able to guarantee salvation to their followers. Whether these denominations identify as Trinitarian or non-Trinitarian, and regardless of their beliefs about the resurrection or the virgin birth, they uniformly promise their adherents salvation.

A significant number of modern Protestant pastors are often cited as having reservations about one or more of the fundamental doctrines that have traditionally defined the Christian faith. At the more radical fringes of this broad movement, there are certain groups that, despite aligning themselves with Protestantism, seem to diverge so far from central Christian tenets that their classification as Christian becomes questionable. This illustrates the remarkable diversity and ambiguity within the Protestant umbrella, reflecting a wide range of beliefs and practices that challenge the notion of a unified Protestant identity.

A striking illustration of a figure whose beliefs deviated drastically from Protestant values is Jim Jones, notorious for the catastrophic events of the 1978 Jonestown massacre in Guyana. Initially, Jones was immersed in the vibrant world of the Pentecostal movement and eventually gained ordination within the mainstream Protestant denomination known as the Christian Church (Disciples of Christ). His organization, the People's Temple, maintained a connection to this Christian denomination despite Jones's unique interpretation of Protestantism, which was heavily infused with communist and socialist ideologies, prioritizing themes of social justice.

Over time, however, Jones distanced himself from traditional Christian teachings, publicly dismissing the Bible and categorizing it as an instrument utilized to marginalize both women and people of color. Within the confines of his commune, he went as far as to declare himself a deity, leading his followers to believe in his divine identity. This transformation from a seemingly devout church leader to a self-proclaimed god showcases the stark contrast between his early mainstream Protestant affiliations and the radical beliefs that ultimately defined his tragic legacy.

Protestantism, with its inherent lack of centralized authority, allowed individuals like Jim Jones, Charles Russell, William Miller, Joseph Smith, and many others to manipulate the faith and steer it down paths dictated by their own ideologies. This unsettling reality was something that Martin Luther himself witnessed before his death in 1546. Less than thirty years after he ignited the Reformation, the troubling potential for distortion within the movement was already glaringly apparent.

While it's not possible to fully chart all the diverse paths Protestantism has taken since Luther's time, I intend to focus on one particular trajectory that has profoundly influenced contemporary liberal American Protestantism. This overview, though necessarily brief, will highlight key moments and developments that together have influenced the complex spiritual landscape we see today. By examining pivotal events and prominent figures, we can trace the intricate journey leading to the various expressions of faith we encounter now, uncovering the fundamental factors that contribute to the overwhelming variety of contemporary synthetic Protestant religions.

All of the post-Reformation religions are synthetic religions. So, what is a synthetic religion? It is a religion that is synthesized and pieced together by using the beliefs of previous religions. We have already established that there are currently around thirty-five thousand different Protestant denominations. If each of these were to originate from an entirely new and disconnected set of ideas, it would be nearly impossible to account for such a vast array of religions and denominations. However, that isn't the case. Throughout the Reformation, there were disagreements among different groups over minor issues, leading to the formation of various subgroups. Importantly, these subgroups didn't emerge in a vacuum; they built upon the foundations of earlier groups, adding or omitting beliefs they deemed to be biblical. Thus, later synthetic religions were built on the blending of existing religious belief systems into a new system.

The Reformation commenced in a structured and traditional fashion, characterized by what is known as the Magisterial Reformation. Key figures such as Martin Luther, Ulrich Zwingli, John Calvin, and other pioneering reformers largely embraced the theological perspectives established by the early church councils and the teachings of the church fathers. However, by the 1520s, shortly after Luther's break in 1517, the initial movement spawned a more radical faction known as the Radical Reformation.

The radicals, driven by an intense desire to redefine Christianity, sought to dismantle all remnants of Catholic doctrine and practice. They fervently believed that the Christian faith had been fundamentally corrupted and needed a complete overhaul. As mentioned earlier, they championed the Great Apostasy theory, which posited that at some pivotal moment—either following the deaths of the apostles or during the reign of Constantine—the original church had entirely deviated from its foundational truths and had ceased to exist in its true form. This bold assertion marked the stark dividing line between the reformers focused on reformation from within traditional Christianity and those advocating for a total break from the past.

From that starting point, with no solid foundations, some of the radicals began to create religions based on their own perceptions of God's fairness. It was almost as though they laid out a bunch of existing religious beliefs on a table, like puzzle pieces, and picked and chose the ones that resonated with them or made sense to their understanding. This resulted in a bunch of wild beliefs that had very short lives and other not-so-wild beliefs that continued to be refined and developed. Among the earliest groups in the Radical Reformation were the Anabaptists, founded in the 1520s. They claimed exclusivity and viewed everyone outside their community as non-Christians, referring to all of Christendom as "The World." They were staunch pacifists, believing that participating in warfare indicated that you were not a real Christian. To handle dissenters within their ranks, they practiced shunning, which involved complete disassociation from the individual. In extreme cases, even spouses were forbidden to speak to one another if one of them was expelled from the community. These practices laid the groundwork for the emergence of other religious groups like the Mennonites and the Amish and also bred various nineteenth-century American imitators, which likewise drew from Anabaptist beliefs.

Unfortunately, they were merely the tip of the innovative "If I were God" iceberg. Approximately thirty years after the Anabaptists, the rationalist strand of the Radical Reformation emerged. Faustus Socinus, the founder of Socinianism, was one of the early figures in this movement. However, Socinus's theological ideas were not entirely his own; he drew heavily from the writings of his uncle, Lelio Socinus. As a result, Socinianism became one of the first synthetic religions of the rationalist strand of the Radical Reformation. The Socinians interpreted Scripture through their own lens, dismissing both the church fathers and established creeds. They denied the Trinity and asserted that Jesus was not divine, and they also denied hell, claiming instead that the soul perishes with the body. They referred to themselves as the brethren—the true brothers in Christ. In 1579, Faustus relocated to Poland, where he took a leadership role in the Minor Reformed Church, known as the Polish Brethren. Socinus successfully converted this movement to align with his theological views. By accepting his rejection of the Trinity in favor of "the oneness of God," the Polish Socinians, or Polish Brethren, became known as Unitarians.

The Polish Socinians, or Polish Brethren, emerged as one of the pioneering groups of the rationalist strand of the Radical Reformation, distinguished by their extreme pacifist beliefs. Their theological framework placed a strong emphasis on reason and critical thinking, encouraging followers to engage deeply with the Scriptures through an analytic, anthropomorphic prism. Their contributions to religious discourse and the dissemination of progressive ideas were vital in advancing their version of Protestantism from that era onward.

The Polish Brethren were a remarkable religious group whose radical commitment to pacifism set them apart from their contemporaries. They emerged as pioneering advocates against both capital punishment and corporal punishment, challenging the prevailing norms of their time with a fervor that was unusual for their society. In addition to their ethical stance on violence, they displayed a profound social consciousness by critiquing the entrenched feudal system that dominated Poland.

Their vision extended to championing the rights of peasants, pushing for their enfranchisement, and advocating for reforms that included universal healthcare and an accessible educational system for all. These progressive ideas were met with significant resistance from the elite, who were deeply invested in maintaining the status quo.

Moreover, the Polish Brethren's theological beliefs further alienated them from mainstream society. Their rejection of the Trinity and the divinity of Christ marked them as proponents of Arianism, a perspective that placed them at odds with the established Catholic and Calvinist authorities. As a result, they faced intense persecution, illustrating the dangers that come with challenging both social and spiritual hierarchies:

> The Warsaw Confederation of 1573 granted religious freedom to Roman Catholics, Lutherans, Calvinists, and Bohemian Brethren, but not to the Arians. . . . In Cracow, the Arians were prone to attacks by Catholic mobs at the instigation of the clergy. . . . [The Polish Brethren left] and moved to the provincial town of Raków . . . [which] became a religious and intellectual center of dissidents. The famous Racovian Academy, established in 1602, provided excellent education not only for fellow believers but also for Catholics and Protestants. . . .
>
>   A period of prosperity for the Polish Brethren ended in 1638 with the closure of the Academy and the confiscation of the printing press. . . . The Arians were expelled from Poland by order of the Sejm (Polish Parliament) in 1658. They moved to the Netherlands, and [continued] their publishing. . . . Although small in numbers

the Arians made a significant impact on political thought in Poland as well as philosophical thought in Western Europe.[9]

In Amsterdam . . . they [took] on the label of Unitarian. . . . Leading figures . . . [decided] that the works of theologians and intellectuals connected with the church should be . . . published. . . . Which they [did] in 1668, with the publication of . . . *The Library of the Polish Brethren*. . . .

The Brethren and their published works are considered to have influenced many Enlightenment thinkers, including John Locke, who owned a complete set of all 9 volumes of [*The Library of the Polish Brethren*]. Isaac Newton, who was privately anti-Trinitarian, also collected many of their works.[10]

During their time in Poland, the Polish Brethren were recognized as one of the most influential intellectual [groups] in the commonwealth, relevant not only in the country, but also abroad. . . .

[Among the] astounding number of intellectuals . . . [who] read and engaged with the movement . . . [was] John Milton, who, during his trial in the Rump Parliament in 1652, was accused of being a member of the religion by Oliver Cromwell.[11]

We have reached a critical juncture in this interconnected series of historical events, marked by a seminal shift. The religious Socinians—who evolved into the Unitarians—began to exert a significant influence on the mostly anti-religious Enlightenment thinkers, who unapologetically propelled the rationalist strand of the Radical Reformation towards a distinctly secular perspective.

Keep in mind that this transformation started with the widespread devastation caused by the plague, which fundamentally altered people's attitudes toward religion and God. A movement emerged to live differently, examining all aspects of life from a human-centered perspective rather than a church-centered one. This initiative aimed to question and challenge the established norms of the existing order, which paved the way for the emergence of the humanist Renaissance, a flourishing of arts and thought that directly contributed to the Magisterial Reformation, which was "partly revival and partly the fruit of humanism."[12] This, in turn, gave rise to the Radical Reformation, which quickly evolved into the rationalist strand of

9. Szkuta, "Arians."
10. Sickafoose, "Four Hundred and Sixty Three," 3, 4.
11. Sobolewski, "Polish Brethren."
12. Gay, *Enlightenment*, 280.

that movement. It is not surprising that this emphasis on rationalism would eventually shape the Enlightenment, a remarkable period also known as the "Age of Reason," where reason and evidence began to take precedence over tradition and faith.

Karen Armstrong, in her bestseller *A History of God*, says that in the Enlightenment era:

> the process of Westernization had begun, and with it, the cult of secularism that claimed independence of God.
>
> They no longer felt that they needed to rely on inherited tradition or even a revelation from God to discover the truth. Intellectuals felt obliged to work out their own theories of religion, starting from scratch.
>
> Proud self-reliance would lead many people to reject the whole idea of a God who reduces [humanity] to the condition of a dependent.[13]

Armstrong succinctly encapsulates the crucial changes in Western thought that marked this period, highlighting the proud secular mindset of the Enlightenment thinkers. The "progressive marginalization of [the Christian] religion"[14] accelerated dramatically as these philosophers viewed the Bible as merely a quaint anthology of fables requiring their enlightened reinterpretation. While they paid lip service to God, suggesting that his attempts to communicate with humanity were inelegant and flawed, they effectively relegated him to the background of their intellectual pursuits. Rejecting his authority, they boldly declared a fresh start, endeavoring to construct rational explanations solely from the heights of their own intellectual prowess. In a grand gesture of allegiance to humanism and the belief in the limitless potential of mankind, they summarily dismissed the notion of human dependency on the divine, positioning themselves as the sole architects of understanding and meaning.

In concert with the prevailing theme explored throughout this book, the title of Peter Gay's extensive examination of that transformative period captures its subsequent ramifications beautifully—*The Enlightenment: The Rise of Modern Paganism*.[15]

---

13. Armstrong, *History of God*, 293, 296, 301.
14. McLeod, *Religious Crisis of the 1960s*, 8.
15. Gay, *Enlightenment*.

HOW DID WE GET HERE?

Peter Gay eloquently showcases his vast and unparalleled scholarly expertise as he delves into the intricate evolution of ideas and concepts in connection with the Enlightenment. His mastery lies not only in the breadth of his understanding but also in his ability to convey complex ideas with clarity and precision.

While it's impossible to provide a fully representative summary of his 550-page book—essential reading for anyone genuinely interested in the topic—the following quotes will offer a glimpse into his insights.

He begins with a pithy summary of the time frame between the plague and the alarming promulgation of the Socinian/Unitarian writings that severely impacted Christian beliefs in just one impactful sentence: "While Christianity was no longer quite the Christianity of the Renaissance, it's worldliness was not yet the secularism of the Enlightenment."[16]

From there, Peter Gay subtly hints at an era characterized by the surprisingly amicable relationships that existed between staunch atheist philosophers and their Christian pagan counterparts. This period was marked by an intriguing exchange of ideas and shared respect despite their fundamentally opposing beliefs: "David Hume, who despised the religious impulse, . . . wrote that Newton, Locke, Clark, etc., being Arians or Socinians, were [at least] sincere. Locke remained a mediator, the last in a long line of pagan Christians. His book, *The Reasonableness of Christianity*, is really a new religion."[17]

He then hits the nail on the head: "The Enlightenment was a derivative, vulgarized restatement of traditional Christian values: a new philosophy; a secularized faith." It was a "rationalist Protestantism."[18]

What predictably followed were allies among the religious elite, as in the case of the Archbishop of Canterbury John Tillotson, whom Voltaire called "the best preacher in Europe" and whose views "delighted deists and skeptics." Unfortunately, the archbishop wasn't alone as, devastatingly, "Liberal Anglicanism and the Deist Enlightenment were connected by a thousand threads."[19]

As stated at the outset, there was no hope of fully capturing the depth and brilliance of Peter Gay's comprehensive book. Nevertheless, these final quotes will serve to reinforce the journey we've taken and illuminate

---

16. Gay, *Enlightenment*, 314.
17. Gay, *Enlightenment*, 319, 320.
18. Gay, *Enlightenment*, 322, 325.
19. Gay, *Enlightenment*, 326, 327.

the path ahead: "Socinianism [is] the ladder on which the 'new theology' climbed." "I have noted how much modern Protestants and [the Enlightenment] philosophers had in common." Even Voltaire "found it easy to praise the rationality of the [Socinian]/Unitarians."[20]

To provide a pithier conclusion to this section of quotes, I'll circle back to the insights of Karen Armstrong: "Christians were on the threshold of a more secular age, though they still adhered to [a] belief in God. The new religion of reason would be known as Deism. It turned its back on traditional mysteries [like] the Trinity. This ideal religion, [by] which man could discover [God] by his own efforts, would, above all, be as simple as possible. The philosophers of the Enlightenment [some of whom kept] the idea of God rejected the cruel God of the Orthodox, who threatened mankind with eternal fire."[21]

Simply put, the philosophers, in their quest for understanding, rejected the God of the Bible in favor of a conception of deity that mirrored their own values. This new interpretation emphasized their own perceptions of fairness, kindness, and love—principles they genuinely felt reflected God's intentions, even though they believed God had not clearly communicated his message. Consequently, they needed to accurately express what God truly meant to convey. This prideful perspective brings us back to the familiar "If I were God . . ." humanist approach to interpreting Scripture, distancing us even further from the biblical Christianity that guided our understanding centuries ago.

It was the logical conclusion of "the four centuries between 1300 and 1700; the prehistory of the Enlightenment. These were centuries when secular forces first expanded and then exploded whatever unity the Christian millennium had possessed. It was the era of pagan Christianity."[22] The influence of pagan Christianity, along with its secular themes, continued to grow and gain traction, particularly in England.

> The [Polish] Brethren certainly [hastened] the development of English Unitarianism. John Biddle, known as the "Father of English Unitarianism," translated several of their publications into English.[23]

20. Gay, *Enlightenment*, 331, 365, 358.
21. Armstrong, *History of God*, 310.
22. Gay, *Enlightenment*, 256.
23. Sickafoose, "Four Hundred and Sixty Three," 4.

These translated Socinian/Unitarian concepts significantly influenced English religious thought, leading to a widespread shift towards Arianism. This intellectual infection spread vigorously through the writings and teachings of rationalists, Enlightenment thinkers, and Deists, who championed reason and individual interpretation of faith. By the close of the eighteenth century, this contagion had permeated the religious landscape so thoroughly that "most Protestant leaders [in] Great Britain preached a sort of deism"[24]—a belief that acknowledged a creator but rejected traditional doctrines and the divinity of Christ.

This divergence in English religious thought paved the way for a series of codified contradictions that crossed the Atlantic and became an integral aspect of the spiritual environment of America. We can now understand the extensive theological and attitudinal evolution of humanism and secular thought that unfolded over centuries, starting with the catastrophic European plague of the fourteenth century and continuing through to America, which was still unknown at the time this story began. This journey reveals how the deviations from traditional Christian beliefs that we have come to adopt are not uniquely ours but rather a confluence of influences shaped by historical events and the rationalist Radical Reformation, Enlightenment, and Deist thinkers.

In America, these innovations were embraced and propagated by many who prioritized their personal interpretations and put their understandings of Christianity above God's. As a result, Socinian/Unitarian/Enlightenment/Deist theologies were rampant in America after the Revolutionary War. In 1805, Harvard had a heavily Unitarian divinity school under Henry Ware. Most of Boston's churches were Unitarian during what was known as the Unitarian controversy of 1805 to 1835. The American Unitarian Association was founded in 1825 and became a potent abolitionist force in the 1850s. William Lloyd Garrison and Ralph Waldo Emerson were both Unitarians.

There had been three Unitarian presidents between 1797 and 1853 (John Adams, John Quincy Adams, and Millard Fillmore). In 1822, Thomas Jefferson said, "I confidently expect Unitarianism [to] become the general religion of the United States."[25] In the aftermath of the American Revolution, Unitarianism began to find its footing as a rational alternative to traditional Christian teachings, thanks in part to its Arian beliefs. Many people

---

24. Wikipedia, "Christianity in the 19th Century."
25. Monticello, "Jefferson's Religious Beliefs."

were drawn to this emerging perspective, pursuing a more open-minded approach to spirituality. One might wonder how such a system could gain popularity, especially since the foundational theological debates surrounding Arianism had seemingly been resolved at the Council of Nicaea in AD 325. Yet, religious innovation in the new nation was marked by a compelling divergence from established creeds, allowing Unitarianism to flourish in a unique and vibrant way.

In the wake of a society that championed freedom of thought, our self-confidence and innovative spirit flourished, particularly in the realm of politics and practical inventions. However, this same environment proved to be highly destructive when it came to religion, as the prominent preacher Jonathan Edwards noted. Reflecting on the American scene in the aftermath of the First Great Awakening, Edwards lamented, "God was withdrawing from us."[26]

In actuality, we were withdrawing from God. The fervor of innovation led individuals, often self-deluded and egotistical, to believe they were uncovering biblical truths that had remained hidden since the time of the apostles. In believing that they were the only ones in the last two millennia to perceive apostolic truths, they had arrogantly untethered themselves from the Christ of the Bible. This mindset was fueled by the so-called "Great Apostasy theory," a concept we have already explored. What they uncovered was not hidden biblical truths or lost teachings of the apostles, but rather a version of Jesus who mirrored their own beliefs and ideals.

Phillip Cary makes this striking observation about these nineteenth-century innovators: "They looked down this well of 19 centuries of dogma, and at the bottom of the well, they saw their own reflection."[27]

By either consciously or unconsciously adjusting the principles of Socinianism/Unitarianism, they could look down the well of centuries of competent theological writings and dismiss them all with a wave of their hand. As Karen Armstrong said earlier, "This ideal religion, [by] which man could discover [God] by his own efforts, would, above all, be as simple as possible."[28] Countless simple men embraced these rational, anthropomorphic concepts because they appealed strongly to their own humanist sensibilities and those of their unsuspecting followers.

---

26. Armstrong, *History of God*, 324.

27. Cary, *History of Christian Theology*, 454 (transcript from lecture 29, "Deism and Liberal Protestantism").

28. Armstrong, *History of God*, 310.

HOW DID WE GET HERE?

An example of this is the aforementioned Dr. John Thomas, who, during the mid-nineteenth century, copied his beliefs from the Socinian/Unitarians to establish his own religion, the Christadelphians. Although he was surrounded by these ideas, which gained popularity after the Revolutionary War with the rise of Unitarianism, Dr. Thomas passed them off as his own. It's clear that he had no understanding of church history. He exported his Christadelphian faith to England, and it spread across Europe.

Notably, the Polish branch of the Christadelphians stands out for its transparency in acknowledging its five hundred–year heritage linked to Socinian/Unitarian thought, a fact that continues to be embraced to this day. It raises an intriguing question about how Dr. Thomas, the American founder of this movement, could have been oblivious to the deep historical roots of the very concepts he championed as his own innovations.

In a previous chapter, we explored how Charles Russell, the founding figure of the Jehovah's Witnesses, deliberately appropriated the teachings of Dr. John Thomas and the Christadelphians, lifting their doctrines word for word. This act of intellectual theft helped him establish his organization in the 1870s, which, up until 1931, was called "The Bible Students." Moving forward to 1934, we see Herbert W. Armstrong drawing heavily from the beliefs and practices of the Jehovah's Witnesses to create the "Worldwide Church of God." Interestingly, the roots of original Adventism also intertwine with these same thematic elements. The simplicity and rationality of these blatantly and undeniably gnostic groups resonated with many, making these faiths particularly appealing to those who were biblically uneducated or unfamiliar with traditional Christian teachings.

The Christadelphians, who uphold their Socinian and Unitarian beliefs, have dwindled to a minimal presence in today's religious landscape, boasting a global membership of fewer than fifty thousand individuals.[29] In recent years, significant shifts have occurred within the other religious groups, notably the Seventh-day Adventists and a faction of the Worldwide Church of God, both of which have adopted Trinitarian views. In stark contrast, Jehovah's Witnesses remain steadfast in their rejection of this Trinitarian doctrine. They continue to undertake a continuous revision of their translation of the Scriptures, striving to align the text with their interpretations and beliefs rather than allowing the teachings to challenge or reshape their understanding of God.

---

29. BBC, "Christadelphians."

The leaders of two of those three groups, Dr. John Thomas and Charles Russell, emerged from the Second Great Awakening Millerite movement, which had a profound influence on virtually every new late nineteenth-century American religion. All three groups continue to guarantee salvation to their members, regardless of their now opposing Trinitarian stances, with the Jehovah's Witnesses still claiming that only their followers will be saved. At the same time, all other professing Christians will be callously annihilated, something, as mentioned, that the Jehovah's Witnesses and their leadership, in their self-righteous indoctrination-euphoria, celebrate at their conventions—as in, "If only those fools had listened to us, the knowledgeable ones, when we knocked on their doors and invited them to join God's only organization and, like us, secure their guaranteed place in the kingdom."

Socinianism/Unitarianism fostered a more rational and innovative mindset towards religion, paving the way for the above groups to challenge traditional beliefs and practices. This shift was instrumental in igniting a significant humanist surge throughout all of American liberal theology, increasingly aligning Christian principles with contemporary intellectual thought. By prioritizing personal interpretation of the Bible over rigid dogmatic frameworks, religious liberals began to reinterpret biblical narratives and teachings.

Up to this point, I have mapped the gradual transformation of Christian attitudes, transitioning away from a deeply God-centered worldview towards one that embraces humanism, individualism, and secularism. This journey, showcasing a more worldly mindset where human experience and agency take center stage, started during the tumultuous era of the fourteenth-century plague and has continued to unfold, reflecting an increasingly anthropogenic approach to theology that often seems capricious and detached from traditional beliefs, persisting into the present day.

After these attitudes became entrenched in the Christian mindset, it is hardly surprising that the Socinian/Unitarian branch of the Reformation would end up shaping dispensationalism, easy-believism, and American Gnosticism nearly as significantly as the antinomian branch of the Reformation, which will be the focus of the next chapter.

CHAPTER 8

UNACCEPTABLE DIVERGENCE

"AGAIN AND AGAIN THROUGHOUT his life [Luther] descended into severe spiritual anxiety and emotional struggle . . . and intense depression. During [one such] period [in 1527], he heard a haunting inner voice that asked him again and again . . . if [he was] leading thousands of people into damning error and breaking the church? At this, said one Luther scholar, 'self-reproach plummeted him into the utter depths of despair.'"[1]

Luther likely recognized early in his reformative journey that if Zwingli could downplay the significance of the Lord's Supper and the Anabaptists could reject the practice of infant baptism, then the concept of private interpretation would proliferate uncontrollably. This shift would open the floodgates for every individual claiming a personal connection to the Spirit, encouraging them to assert their own interpretations of Scripture as the definitive truth. In this tumultuous landscape, every traditional Christian doctrine would become vulnerable to reinterpretation by various factions or individuals. By initiating this movement, Luther inadvertently provided a pathway for countless Protestants to believe that they possessed the "correct" revelation of faith, thus claiming the authority to assert their unique understanding of Scripture as its authentic meaning.

Furthermore, in the wake of the Peasant's Revolt, it must have been clear to him that without the backing of state churches wielding power, a pastor's authority might likely depend on his congregation's willingness to embrace his teachings—often influenced by beliefs not rooted in Scripture. In essence, the members of the flock would assess the pastor's

1. "Martin Luther's Anfechtungen."

interpretations by contrasting them with their personal perceptions of what they deemed to be the will of a "fair God."

The allure of low-quality, simplistic humanist theology lies in its ability to resonate with the lowest common denominator, appealing to those seeking easy answers. Many insightful commentators have pointed out that if humans could fully comprehend the limitless and unfathomable nature of God using their finite understanding, it would fundamentally undermine their reason for worshiping him. This observation serves as a poignant critique of those who desire a deity that aligns comfortably with their overly simplistic, childlike theological constructs.

Protestant author Wyatt Houtz expresses an observable truth when he states, "The Reformation opened Pandora's box, resulting in a chain reaction of church schisms that have produced 38,000 or more Protestant denominations today." He then goes on to comment on the writings of a freethinking Catholic theologian who, in 1979, was removed from the faculty of the University of Tübingen in Germany by Pope John Paul II for his public questioning of the doctrine of papal infallibility—as well as Catholic Mariology. Houtz states that he wrote this article because he believes that "this is an important time for Protestants [like himself] to listen to these criticisms."[2]

Having already examined the context surrounding four of the seven criticisms outlined by Houtz, I won't be venturing into new territory by sharing Küng's insights on these particular points. He presents his thoughts on the previously covered topics of Zwingli, Thomas Müntzer, the Peasants' Revolt, and lastly, Erasmus.

> Martin Luther was a *demonizer*: Hans Küng writes, "How was it that in every opponent (and *not* just the pope) he literally saw the devil?"
>
> Martin Luther was a *fanatical biblicist*: Hans Küng writes, "When the fanatical *enthusiasts*, Karlstadt and Thomas Münzer at their head, invoked their personal interpretation of Scripture, as opposed to Luther's, and the Holy Spirit, hadn't Luther vigorously denied them *the freedom of a Christian man* he had claimed for himself?"
>
> Martin Luther was a *warmonger*: Hans Küng writes, "Didn't Luther have a share of the guilt for the *Peasants' Revolt*, which swept through the German Empire, together with its catastrophic

2. Houtz, "Martin Luther's Share."

consequences? When the peasants rose up in revolution in southwestern Germany, at first demanding only the rights that the nearby Swiss had long enjoyed, hadn't Luther left them in the lurch? Indeed, hadn't he driven them into death and misery when he hotheadedly incited the princes *Against the Murderous and Thieving Hordes of the Peasants* (1525), goading them to pitiless, blood measures?"

Martin Luther was *vehemently wrathful*: Hans Küng writes, "And finally hadn't the man from Wittenberg also *fallen like a wild beast* on him, on Erasmus, who had argued patiently and calmly—in academic style—with Luther? Although Erasmus' arguments for human freedom and responsibility were really well grounded in Scripture, hadn't Luther reviled him as a dolt, a freethinker, and a skeptic, as a new pagan, a despiser of Scripture, an enemy of Christianity, and a destroyer of religion?"[3]

Would Martin Luther regard each of the founders behind today's thousands of Protestant denominations as demonic figures, akin to how he viewed Zwingli? Would he deny them the very right of theological interpretation that he himself passionately advocated for, just as he did to Thomas Münzer? Would he endorse the violent suppression of all Protestant factions whose beliefs incited bloodshed, reminiscent of his stance during the Peasants' War? Lastly, would he reject any meaningful dialogue with dissenters, dismissing their arguments as foolish and labeling them as pagans or enemies of Christianity, much like he did with Erasmus?

While the answers to those questions remain uncertain, what is clear is Luther's strong condemnation of antinomianism. Johann Agricola, who would later embrace antinomianism, was a "friend of Martin Luther . . . [who] accompanied him as recording secretary to his Leipzig debate of 1519 with the scholar Johann Eck. In 1525, Agricola helped introduce Lutheranism to Frankfurt and, in the same year, became head of the Latin school at Eisleben. There, he began to assert his antinomianism (Greek *anti*, "against"; *nomos*, "law"), condemning the law as an unnecessary carry-over from the Old Testament" and asserting that "Christians are freed by grace from the need to obey the Ten Commandments."[4]

---

3. Points 3, 4, 5, and 7 from the section "Seven Ways Martin Luther Shares the Guilt for the Reformation in Houtz, "Martin Luther's Share"; emphasis in original.

4. Encyclopedia Britannica, "Johann Agricola."

FAKE SALVATION IN MODERN GNOSTIC AMERICA

In 1539, Luther responded to Agricola's antinomianism by publishing *A Treatise Against Antinomians*. Luther stated that he had "pressed [Agricola] to publish an open recantation," which he later did.[5]

In the following section of the treatise, Luther outlines the challenges he has encountered as a result of various opposing factions, with the antinomians representing the most recent opposition: "I alone ... have undergone more than twenty several storms and sects [from the Devil]. The first was the *Papacy*. ... And when I was almost freed of the fear of these devilish whirlwinds, another [storm of the] devil breaks in upon me [the Peasants' Revolt]. ... After this came the *Anabaptists*." He notes also Servetus and Campanus, and the "*Antinomians*, who abolish the Law."[6]

Despite the stern disapproval voiced by Martin Luther and the subsequent recantation of Johann Agricola, antinomianism has proven to be a remarkably persistent ideology, resurging with regularity throughout the annals of Christian history. A new set of visionaries often spearheads each revival—individuals convinced that they have uncovered divine truths overlooked by the mainstream. These men ingeniously craft elaborate and seemingly credible scriptural justifications for their beliefs.

Over time, their interpretations morph into what they believe to be a fresh theological system, though it is fundamentally rooted in the previously discredited ideas of antinomianism. These reimagined doctrines frequently find their way into the hands of ambitious pastors—individuals who are eager to harness this well-trodden gnostic church growth formula to fuel their popularity and further their own agendas. They, too, believe they possess insights that have eluded others.

This recurring historical trend of gnostic, antinomian, easy-believism, which offers worthless guarantees of salvation while pretending to be Christian, was revitalized in America through the writings of John Nelson Darby and the Plymouth Brethren. As with Mormonism, Millerism, Adventism, and the Jehovah's Witnesses, nineteenth-century America also provided fertile ground for the growth of antinomian dispensationalism, where the interplay between personal liberty and a semblance of divine grace found acceptance among both pastors and parishioners, who were eager to embrace fresh and innovative spiritual ideas. In this arrangement, as at all other times of gnostic, antinomian intrusion, the only real casualties were Christ and the integrity of his gospel.

5. Luther, "Treatise Against Antinomians."
6. Luther, "Treatise Against Antinomians"; emphasis in original.

The dispensational antinomian system enjoyed a period of significant growth and widespread acceptance, thriving on the foundational beliefs that had been cultivated over generations. However, as I previously noted, the cultural normalization of homosexuality led to the homosexual Christian community wielding the "behavior doesn't matter" gospel against the very dispensational churches that had championed that theology for over a century and a half. This led to the physical division of many of these churches due to the unraveling of theological cohesion.

As the rift deepened, dispensational pastors faced a critical crossroads, compelled to confront a stark choice. They would either have to honestly admit that the entire system is a fraud, or they would have to hypocritically announce that most heterosexual behavior doesn't matter, but all homosexual behavior does. As pointed out earlier, a straightforward acknowledgment of the obvious would put an end to all forms of salvation offered through radio broadcasts, TV ministries, church altar calls, or any entrenched mainstream practice that awards salvation to people you know nothing about.

It appears that numerous dispensational pastors have opted for the latter path, which is both obviously contradictory and morally questionable yet cannily pragmatic in its approach. These leaders have woven a narrative that sacrifices integrity for perceived practicality. In contrast, a courageous few have chosen the path of honesty, openly acknowledging that the entire dispensational framework they had operated within has been a deception from the very beginning. Non-dispensationalists also chimed in.

In his amusingly titled November 2023 book, *How Dispensationalism Got Left Behind*, Daniel Hummel shares his thoughts on the subject. Hummel's provocative title raises intriguing questions about the legacy of dispensationalism. In August 2023, he participated in an engaging discussion with Albert Mohler, the president of the Southern Baptist Theological Seminary in Louisville, Kentucky. They explored several important themes from the book. Below are some of the key highlights from their conversation.

"'The Rise and Fall of Dispensationalism'—A Conversation with Daniel Hummel"

Hummel begins the discussion by taking us back to the 1830s where we meet John Nelson Darby, an Anglican priest recognized as the founder of dispensationalism.⁷ Building on this footing, he weaves a narrative that also references William Miller and his movement (mentioned earlier in the book), portraying Miller as a significant predecessor. Miller's 1840s predictions regarding the end times reflect a form of millenarianism, which can be loosely seen as having laid some of the conceptual groundwork for dispensationalism.

Darby's initial training as an Anglican priest becomes all the more intriguing when we reflect on what was discussed in the preceding chapter, "How Did We Get Here." In our investigation, we traced the intricate history of nineteenth-century American churches back to the Socinians, a group that evolved into the Unitarians in Poland. After their expulsion in 1658, they established an extensive network for their writings in the Netherlands, where Socinian texts profoundly shaped the intellectual landscape, influencing Enlightenment thinkers, Deists, and various English churches.

Specifically, the impact of the Unitarians on the Anglican Church was substantial, prompting some Anglicans to reevaluate the traditional doctrine of the Trinity. This Unitarian influence motivated the Anglican Church to embark on a journey toward reason, individual liberty, and rational thought. In a more practical and tangible way, the Unitarians played a pivotal role in altering the Anglican prayer book, leading to many Unitarian congregations today adopting a Unitarian version of the *Book of Common Prayer* for their worship services.

Boston's King's Chapel, a distinguished national historic landmark today, was established as an Anglican church before transforming into the first Unitarian church in America around 1787. The common threads between Socinianism, Unitarianism, rationalism, Deism, and Anglicanism created an environment of acceptance for all of the nineteenth-century American religious innovators. In such a fertile setting, it is little wonder that John Nelson Darby found the ideal conditions for his new system to take root.

Mohler then reflects on the complexities of the entire dispensational system and shares his astonishment at a specific educational approach adopted by both its educators and their supporters: "What's amazing to me is that there were so many conservative Christians who gave themselves to becoming more or less self-taught and conference-taught experts in this system."⁸

---

7. This section draws heavily from Mohler, "Rise and Fall of Dispensationalism."
8. Mohler, "Rise and Fall of Dispensationalism."

UNACCEPTABLE DIVERGENCE

Mohler really hits the nail on the head here. Even the most highly educated pastors who have emerged from this movement often became tunnel blind and self-righteously confident in their beliefs. This is mainly because they tend to be self-taught or rely on conference-driven teachings that focus entirely on their specific system and not on the whole of established Christian history and theology. Older synthetic religions, certainly the Magisterial ones, at least required a cursory study of the previous religions they opposed, if only to highlight their own distinguishing features. When you consider your own nineteenth-century framework as both the beginning and end of Christian theology while dismissing all prior thought as misguided, you end up missing out on a balanced theological viewpoint and even a basic understanding of Christian history. This void was noted previously in the case of Dr. John Thomas. He, like modern dispensational pastors, lacked awareness of earlier theological developments, which is why he failed to realize that his system was merely a revival of Socinianism.

Dispensationalists essentially hold that their nineteenth-century interpretation is the only valid one. This mindset results in the belief that their insights are the sole credible understanding, effectively dismissing any previous knowledge as irrelevant. This mindset has created a barrier to meaningful dialogue. Those who are well-versed in comprehensive Christian theology and history and attempt to introduce these perspectives in discussions are often dismissed as outdated or ignorant. Conversely, those self-contained, echo chamber, modern gnostic dispensationalists who, like all gnostics throughout Christian history, insist that they alone hold the truth, effectively place themselves beyond conversation and rational debate. The echo chamber they had built was disrupted by the rise of the homosexual community, which cleverly used their own tactics against them. This marked a much-needed turning point, forcing dispensationalists to confront the shaky foundation of their beliefs. As their framework began to unravel, some realized that their unwavering confidence in its validity was nothing more than an exercise in mutual reinforcement and collective self-deception.

Mohler and Hummel then embark on a highly constructive and insightful conversation.[9]

---

9. Quotes throughout this overview of the Mohler and Hummel conversation are from Mohler, "Rise and Fall."

FAKE SALVATION IN MODERN GNOSTIC AMERICA

Hummel notes, "What we see today is a popular version [of Darby's system, adapted] for a more consumer-oriented Christian culture that sort of assumes a dispensationalist background."

Hummel seems to be describing one of the ubiquitous pop culture, music-heavy services held weekly on consumer-friendly church stages, supported by the theological backdrop of dispensationalism. This brings to mind an earlier chapter where we referred to "entertainment centers masquerading as churches," and A. W. Tozer stating, "The old Cross slew men; the new cross entertains them. The old Cross condemned; the new cross amuses."[10]

In the United Kingdom, significant and innovative religious changes are happening that Mohler believes many Americans are unaware of. At the same time, a surge of spiritual zeal is sweeping through the United States, primarily fueled by "the Second Great Awakening. It set loose all these sects and cults, so many of them from the American Northeast, and everybody had a system, whether it was Mary Baker Eddy or Joseph Smith."

Hummel then remarks that in "the late 19th century, new developments in Protestantism [were] ripping apart or at least leading to a major critique of assumed Biblical authority. There [was] definitely an appetite for people like Darby to come along to create a modern way of approaching the Bible, one that [used] a language of linear time and [divided] things up very cleanly to show that the Bible can sort of be as modern as any of these other things that are trying to critique the Bible."

Darby did not fit the description of a literalist, a term often linked to dispensationalism today, which implies a straightforward or historical-grammatical interpretation of the text. In fact, Darby was quite the opposite: "He saw typologies on almost every page of the Bible and dozens of them sometimes, and actually, Scofield did as well."

Religious zeal is setting "loose all these sects and cults," and everyone, including Darby, has "a system." Biblical authority is purposely being ripped apart, and that's generating "an appetite for people like Darby to come along to create a modern way of approaching the Bible." There's a troubling lack of thoughtful consideration for more theologically sound alternatives, replaced instead by a fervent, almost fanatical, mindset of discarding the old in favor of the new. In this context, Darby and, later, Scofield serve as key proponents, providing the intellectual ammunition for this assault on tradition. They move away from a strict adherence to

---

10. Tozer, *Radical Cross*, 174.

long-established interpretation, replacing rigorous theological inquiry with the concept of typologies. These typologies, as broad classifications, grant creative individuals the freedom to construct their own narratives. It's not surprising that the book of Revelation, rich in metaphorical language and ripe for endless allegorical interpretation, becomes a foundational pillar of dispensationalism.

"Dispensationalists really were about building a movement, about building an entire intellectual, theological complex, an ecosystem that would support not just the defense of their views but the perpetuation of them for generation after generation. They had, over the early 20th century, built the Bible Institute movement. Many of the Bible institutes that we take for granted today as Christian colleges and universities were built by dispensationalists."

Throughout this period, various journals, presses, and publishers collaborated to promote dispensationalist theology. Their objective was to solidify a specific viewpoint and impose the dispensationalist perspective "on nearly every aspect of theology." They were likewise quite passionate about promoting dispensationalism "in terms of convincing you of the system."

Hummel points out that Dallas Seminary in Dallas, Grace Theological Seminary in Winona Lakes, Indiana, and Talbot Seminary produced countless pastors who were educated in the dispensational framework.

"This was one of the parts of the story that I really wanted to highlight. [There] was [a] massive amount of, I guess for lack of a better term, scholarship that you could find mid-century produced by dispensationalists, the hundreds of dissertations and thousands of articles in different journals." Certainly, it would be tedious to review all of that, but it all represents a project that was very deliberate.

Individuals like Lewis Sperry Chafer, who founded Dallas Seminary, were instrumental in shaping the movement. His own influence extended particularly through his students and those he mentored at Dallas, such as John Walvoord, who played a key role in leading the seminary for many years. Additionally, as previously noted in this book, Charles Ryrie stands out as a crucial figure in systematic theology within dispensationalism, having published a notable work titled *Dispensationalism Today* in 1965.

On the opposite side of the fundamentalist-modernist debate stands Gresham Machen, whose book, *Christianity and Liberalism*, was released in 1923. "In that book, . . . he makes the very . . . accurate assessment that theological liberalism is not another form of Christianity. It is a heresy. . . . Christianity and liberalism [are] two different religions."

Noting that Machen is a Presbyterian, Hummel then discusses how a group of Presbyterians voiced their disagreement, leading Machen to establish Westminster Theological Seminary. Throughout the 1930s, 1940s, and 1950s, this seminary played a pivotal role in opposing dispensationalism. "Dallas and Westminster debate over [whether] dispensationalism is a modern heresy. Is it valid?"

Mohler highlights a contradiction among some Dispensationalists who assert that "the Church has always believed [the fundamental tenets of dispensationalism]." At the same time, they also claim that these truths were rediscovered in the nineteenth century. He subsequently emphasizes the obvious truth that "you can't have it both ways. You can't say the Church has always believed this and we just rediscovered this in the 19th century. You have got to take one of those arguments or the other, which is one of the points that Machen and his colleagues made to the fundamentalists and the dispensationalists."

Continuing on, Mohler says, "[There are] two more parts to our story here. . . . One of them is what now appears in retrospect to have been kind of a false mountaintop experience for . . . the success of dispensationalism in the United States. It was [misleading to measure the overall success of the movement by the marketing accomplishments of] Tim LaHaye and The Left Behind series. If you were just looking at book sales, popular evangelicalism . . . , dispensationalism would have looked like the coming thing, not the going thing, so what happened there?"

Hummel also points out that around 1970 "there's just massive appeal for a popularized, really trendy [movement]. That's what Late Great Planet Earth was, [a] trendy version of the end times scenario." Later, "people like Chuck Smith, the Calvary Chapel founder, speculated about 1983 among other dates [for the rapture]." From the eighties into the nineties, Smith and others dealt "sort of successive blows to the credibility of dispensationalism as a theological system."

Hummel also says that "one of the sad things [was] seeing someone like John Walvoord, who was this sort of stately theologian running Dallas Seminary. He got in on the pop dispensationalism game with his [bestselling book] *Armageddon Oil in the Middle East*. He published that in 1974, right after the Arab-Israeli War in 1973."

UNACCEPTABLE DIVERGENCE

The key highlights in the concluding section of quotes delve into the reasons behind the widespread acceptance and influence of the dispensational system. Essentially, a theological industrial complex emerged, characterized by a network of institutions, publications, and influential figures that collectively shaped and promoted this framework of thought, embedding it deeply within the fabric of American religious discourse.

"Dispensationalists really were about building a movement," backed by influential intellectuals who crafted a supportive "ecosystem" to ensure the longevity of their views across generations. Their journals and publications aimed to reinforce the dispensationalist perspective "on nearly every aspect of theology." They were intent on "convincing you of the system," sure that most would back down when browbeaten and pressured by esteemed institutions like Dallas Seminary, Grace Theological Seminary, and Talbot Seminary. This initiative was supported by a committed group of hundreds of pastors educated within the dispensational structure. Who could possibly stand up and hold firmly to biblical truths in the face of such overwhelming force from what could, for lack of a better term, be called "scholarship"? Their relentless, multifaceted approach was conscious and deliberate.

Their leadership was impressive, articulate, and unwavering. Organizations like Dallas Seminary, guided by Lewis Sperry Chafer, brought in devoted disciples such as John Walvoord and gifted writers like Charles Ryrie. Meanwhile, Gresham Machen raised a warning, labeling "dispensationalism a modern heresy." Yet his voice seemed to get lost amid the chorus of enthusiasm surrounding the system. Later dissenters found themselves even more overwhelmed when attempting to contest the simplistic and appealing narrative spun by Tim LaHaye and the Left Behind series.

Darby and, later, Scofield offered what they assured would be an enthralling odyssey into the rediscovery of profound theological heights. This venture beckoned both pastors and congregants alike to embrace the tempting illusion of easy-believism, wrapped in the seductive promise of guaranteed gnostic salvation. Almost universally, individuals eagerly and thoughtlessly jumped on the bandwagon and "got in on the pop dispensationalism game." Those who embarked on this extended spiritual journey would eventually realize that the decades of religious ecstasy they experienced were nothing more than a "false mountaintop experience." Ultimately, the fundamental shortcomings of the system they had put their faith in would be dramatically exposed. So, in the end, both they and the concept of dispensationalism "got left behind."

Next are the thoughts of one of the courageous few who have chosen the path of brutal honesty, openly acknowledging that the entire dispensational framework they had operated within has been a deception from the very beginning. Steve Gregg, whose insights on hell were referenced in an earlier chapter, wrote a thought-provoking article in 2015 titled "Is Dispensationalism Indispensable?"

> Many Christians today read Scripture through a theological paradigm that was unknown prior to the nineteenth century.[11]

Gregg then explains the foundational concepts of dispensationalism, explicitly focusing on the rapture, tribulation, and millennium. He emphasizes many of the points previously discussed regarding how this movement gained traction through Bibles, novels, notable figures, and, crucially, the prominent dispensational seminaries. These combined efforts ultimately led to the establishment of these beliefs as the "official doctrine" for nearly all of American conservative Evangelicalism. Initially regarded with skepticism, dispensationalism ultimately gained acceptance, and for many, its foundational assumptions came to be seen as essential for accurate biblical interpretation.

He reinforces the point that it's another of the brand-new nineteenth-century religious systems. As an innovative new system emerging amid a sea of other new systems, it was understandably met with a degree of skepticism.

"Like many American evangelicals, I was once a dispensationalist without knowing it."[12] His instructors failed to tell him that they were teaching him to understand the Bible using a conceptual framework that had been developed just under one hundred and fifty years prior. "I had no inclination to investigate the relative merits of my system against those of any other—simply because I didn't know there was anything to investigate. I had the impression that ours was the only way sensible people had ever viewed Scripture. In other words, I was not educated but indoctrinated." It was only through his personal exploration of Scripture that he was prompted to reevaluate certain facets of his beliefs, which made him realize the extent of his indoctrination.

11. Gregg, "Is Dispensationalism Indispensable?"
12. Gregg, "Is Dispensationalism Indispensable?"

UNACCEPTABLE DIVERGENCE

Steve Gregg, like many now sorting through their own dispensational beliefs in 2025, came to a profound realization: "I was not educated but indoctrinated." This realization is similar to the journeys of many devoted dispensationalists who are reconsidering what they once believed to be unquestionable biblical truths. Gregg once firmly believed that the interpretations he held were "the only way sensible people had ever viewed Scripture." However, something shifted within him, prompting an unexpected insight—one that seemingly eluded both the leaders and followers of Jehovah's Witnesses and contemporary dispensationalists alike. He pondered a refreshing idea: Why not examine these new concepts against the unyielding standard of the Bible?

Gregg notes that dispensationalism "was introduced by [a nineteen-year-old student,] John Nelson Darby (1800–1882)."[13] This fact must have slipped his mind during the many years he uncritically adhered to his dispensational teachings.

Gregg then discusses Darby's narrow fixation on a supposed future time when God will fulfill his Old Testament promises to Israel. After this, he shares his thoughts on the "Great Apostasy" theory, a staple of pseudo-religious nineteenth-century America. In alignment with that, Gregg emphasizes Darby's claims regarding his "rediscovered truth."

I have previously detailed the intriguing parallels between nineteenth-century cults and dispensationalism and would like to expand on that analysis with several additional points worthy of consideration. Like the Jehovah's Witnesses and the Mormons, John Nelson Darby operated within the narrative framework of the Great Apostasy theory, asserting that he had "rediscovered" long-lost truths. It's the same script, as Darby's claim conveys the identical strong sense of urgency and revelation, reflecting the passionate infatuation seen in those other two movements, for all three claimed to recover what they perceived as lost divine knowledge.

Also, like Charles Russell, John Nelson Darby made his "discoveries" at just nineteen years of age while attending a mainstream Protestant college. Instead of absorbing and learning from his teachers and their vast knowledge of the entirety of theological scholarship, he audaciously injected his own unqualified belief that there would eventually be a time when God would literally bring to fruition his Old Testament promises to Israel.

The parallels I've drawn between dispensationalists and Jehovah's Witnesses are far more pronounced than I initially realized. These connections

---

13. Gregg, "Is Dispensationalism Indispensable?"

are not simply coincidental; instead, they reveal a deeper intertwining of beliefs. Jehovah's Witnesses represent a distinct and nuanced branch of dispensationalism, drawing upon the same innovative interpretations of biblical prophecy and eschatological themes. Their shared perspectives illuminate the intricacies of their theological frameworks, highlighting how both groups engage with Scripture in unique yet overlapping ways.

This affiliation stems from their emphasis on God's kingdom, the fulfillment of spiritual promises, and many other parallels. After Charles Russell stole all of the Christadelphian tenets word for word, and also appropriated aspects of adventism, he then expanded the theology of his "one true church" by unabashedly pilfering ideas from Darby. Their similarities are outlined in an insightful article by Gary DeMar from The American Vision website. Noting that the front page of a Jehovah's Witness magazine asked, "Are We Living in the Last Days?" DeMar goes on to say,

> This is the same title that I used for a series of talks I gave on Bible prophecy many years ago. My answer was "no," and still is. The Jehovah's Witnesses give an emphatic "yes." The JWs have been in the last-days-business for more than a century.
> The JWs follow an end-time scenario that is not much different from the one outlined in the Left Behind series and in so many books dealing with Bible prophecy.[14]

In the article, DeMar proceeds to list similarities between Jehovah's Witnesses and dispensationalists, particularly in their eschatological beliefs. Both groups interpret current global events—such as armed conflicts, the rise of terrorism, natural disasters like devastating tsunamis, and widespread health crises including malaria, influenza, and AIDS—as significant indicators that the end times are drawing near. Furthermore, they maintain a shared conviction that the cataclysmic event known as Armageddon is still imminent, suggesting that these occurrences are not just random but rather fulfill prophetic warnings about the impending conclusion of the world as we know it. This alignment in interpretation underscores a profound sense of urgency and a call to preparedness that characterizes the teachings of both groups.

> Everything I heard, except for a few odd translations of passages that come from their idiosyncratic New World Translation, are the same types of arguments I get from dispensationalists daily. Of

---

14. DeMar, "Jehovah's Witnesses."

course, there are some notable differences, but the overall apologetic is nearly identical.[15]

Given that both movements share a comparable dispensational framework, emerged in tumultuous nineteenth-century America, and assert their unique perspectives as the singular truth, this raises intriguing questions about the extent of their apparent theological cross-pollination. Conceived by self-proclaimed visionaries bearing the naivety often found in nineteen-year-olds, one must ponder whether it is sheer coincidence that both have nurtured an unbiblical, malleable, and fervently fanatical following. Is it possible that the assurance of guaranteed salvation, paired with a deep-seated sense of group exceptionalism and subtle yet powerful indoctrination techniques, creates a recipe for turning individuals into unsuspecting, gullible followers who cling to their beliefs despite any evidence from the Bible that contradicts them?

Back to Steve Gregg: "Darby acknowledged that his system represented a departure from historic Christian theology."[16] As mentioned earlier, the system initially faced skepticism and criticism from those who clung to historical truths that contradicted Darby's so-called "rediscovered" truths. It has become increasingly evident that many of these so-called truths were, in fact, not truths at all.

Darby saw his system as a "rediscovered truth," just like Jehovah's Witnesses, Mormons, Adventists, and the litany of cults that exploded onto the scene in nineteenth-century America. The freedoms cherished in the United States, combined with a pervasive sense of spiritual exceptionalism, transformed the nation into a breeding ground for the emergence of cults and appealingly simplistic frameworks of biblical distortions and deception.

Unlike Jehovah's Witnesses, Mormons, and Seventh-day Adventists, John Nelson Darby's theological perspectives had been viewed as historically and doctrinally consistent within Christian theology until recently. His emphasis on the pre-tribulation rapture and a literal interpretation of biblical prophecy has garnered significant attention and acceptance in evangelical circles over the last hundred and fifty years.

"Darbyism . . . became popular in the United States through a variety of media [and through seminaries and publications], not least of which was the publication of the Scofield Reference Bible in 1909." Scofield's notes,

---

15. DeMar, "Jehovah's Witnesses."
16. Gregg, "Is Dispensationalism Indispensable?"

printed at the bottom of each page, offered dispensational interpretations of the related biblical passages. This publication significantly impacted numerous evangelical readers, "who often read Scofield's notes as though they carried some kind of canonical authority due to their placement on the pages of Scripture."[17]

I have previously articulated comparable concepts in earlier sections of the book. It's also worth noting that Scofield's notes create an impression of possessing "some kind of canonical authority due to their placement on the pages of Scripture." The Jehovah's Witnesses take this notion a step further by boldly asserting that their leadership has served as the direct voice of Jesus Christ since 1919, and thus, their monthly magazine is studied in lieu of the Bible. While dispensationalists are more subtle and Jehovah's Witnesses overt, both strategies are designed to cultivate the perception that challenging their theology equates to challenging God. Followers of both groups seem to sincerely believe that their belief system is, in a very real sense, synonymous with the Bible and God. Consequently, questioning their group or its theology is viewed as equivalent to questioning God himself, and disloyalty to the group is portrayed as a rejection of God.

> Some of the issues affected have a more practical bearing on the daily Christian life. According to Ryrie, "The church is not a part of this kingdom at all." According to dispensationalism, the gospel preached by Jesus was the gospel of the Kingdom of God and was intended for the Jews. A new dispensation, the Church Age, has intervened, introducing another gospel: "the gospel of grace"—which was first preached by Paul. According to Ryrie, "The apostle Paul was principally, though not exclusively, the agent of the revelation of the grace of God for this dispensation." It is Paul's gospel that we are to be preaching today. Only after the rapture of the church (the close of the present dispensation) will the gospel of the kingdom again be relevant.[18]

Similar to gnostics throughout history, nineteenth-century American gnostics such as Russell and Darby placed great emphasis on the writings of Paul. This focus aligns with the points I discussed in my book *The Battle for the Divinity of Christ in the Early Centuries*, as the following demonstrates:

> Interestingly, the [Valentinian] Gnostics, like the Marcionite [gnostics], also found the writings of Paul very useful in supporting their

17. Gregg, "Is Dispensationalism Indispensable?"
18. Gregg, "Is Dispensationalism Indispensable?"

theology. Paul's writings are complicated; and obviously, the more complicated the writing, the more subject it is to self-promoting interpretation. Peter warned that "[Paul's] letters contain some things that are hard to understand, which ignorant and unstable people distort, as they do other Scriptures, to their own destruction" (2 Pet 3:16 NIV). Just as Justin Martyr omitted Paul's letters from his own writings because of how the Marcionites had been using them, author James Dunn states that Tertullian later called Paul "the apostle of the heretics" because of how the Gnostics had been using his words. He goes on to say that "Paul's writings were attractive to the Gnostics [when] interpreted in the Gnostic way."[19]

Gregg wrote his article in 2015, before the full church-dividing impact of the mainstreaming of homosexuality took hold, forcing dispensational antinomian pastors to reassess and modify their foundational beliefs. However, when he discusses the implications for everyday Christian life and refers to Ryrie's view that the New Testament gospel was intended solely for the Jews, he is undoubtedly touching on the topic of dispensational antinomianism. Ryrie's dispensational antinomianism is also plainly evident when he mentions "the gospel of grace."

Clearly, the Jehovah's Witnesses, Mormons, and dispensationalists are all part of the litany of innovative new religions that exploded onto the scene in nineteenth-century America. Darby's "rediscovered truth," like Jehovah's Witness and Mormon "rediscovered truths," should be discarded, not disjointedly repaired. The modifications being implemented by dispensational pastors and churches are an inventive tidying up of their theology or, as I said earlier, an attempt to backfill the vintage dispensational landscape with subterfuge. It seems that pastors are increasingly preoccupied with fine-tuning their language and rephrasing their explanations, attempting to portray complete reversals in doctrine and theology as mere minor adjustments.

This approach conveniently overlooks the reality that for decades, they have used the pulpit to spread false and unbiblical narratives. While these leaders may make adjustments to their terminology and teachings, they fail to address the core issue: the entrenched, misleading illusion of guaranteed salvation that they offer their followers. By continuing to assure congregants of their salvation, they are perpetuating this troubling facade.

This approach not only undermines genuine understanding but also constitutes a disturbing form of fraud and deception, leaving the faithful

---

19. Carranza, *Battle for the Divinity*, 21.

potentially misled about their spiritual safety. If dispensational churchgoers still believe that aspect of their own dispensational indoctrination, which most do, they will find themselves under no compulsion to rethink their theology, as Steve Gregg did on his pilgrimage away from dispensationalism and toward spiritual truth. His awakening began with a stark recognition: he suddenly realized just how deeply he had been indoctrinated, prompting him to explore the idea that the truths Darby had "rediscovered" might not be truths at all.

The entire theological framework he had accepted as truth had originated from the mind of a nineteen-year-old heretic who had conjured a concoction of ideas from his own imagination, leading Gregg to firmly reject it. In the context of those who savor the false eternal security aspect of dispensationalism, they would have to be incredibly self-deceiving to think, "Even though the system is a sham, I like the part where they promised me salvation. So, I'll just hold onto that belief and continue to embrace it." That would be like a Mormon leaving the Church of Latter-day Saints (LDS) and rejecting it as a fraud but keeping the part where he believes he is going to be the god of his own little planet, or a Jehovah's Witness rejecting the Watchtower organization yet still believing he is one of the 144,000 anointed from the book of Revelation.

In both scenarios, individuals make a deliberate choice to separate themselves from widespread deceit, all the while clinging to a promise that has offered them a reassuring sense of Mormon or Watchtower security in the afterlife—a comfort they have cherished for decades. Absurd? However, adherents of dispensationalism are striving to conveniently delude themselves into doing the same thing.

As detailed in earlier chapters, there's no such thing as the certainty of salvation. Also discussed was the fact that only on the very last day will Jesus himself disclose a possibility that no human alive had the ability to know. In Matt 7:11, Jesus himself unveils the final possibility, which has been completely invisible to all human eyes. When we cry out to him, "Lord, Lord," we will believe wholeheartedly that we are true Christians; yet, it may turn out that all along, we had only "demonic faith."

Moreover, if dispensationalists upheld the conviction that they alone among Protestant denominations held the exclusive truth of Christian theology and all others were wrong—an understanding they would have to believe was divinely imparted to John Nelson Darby by the Holy Spirit—then that might at least allow for those fanatically committed to the system to start evaluating their standing in light of the other conditions that might influence their sense of security. However, this narrative, asserting that dispensationalism represents both the beginning and the end of Christian theology, has been thoroughly and conclusively dismantled. As a result, the very first foundation upon which the certainty of salvation rests has crumbled, leaving no credible basis for dispensational assurance.

As was detailed and extensively clarified in an earlier chapter, Andreas Bergman's extraordinary thesis begins by using the term "The Protestant Dilemma," which he explains in the following words:

> Luther's thought assumes that if one wants to be infallibly certain of his salvation, they must be certain that their interpretation of the Bible is infallibly correct. Obviously, the concern that false exegesis threatens the certainty of salvation explains why Luther opposed Zwingli's doctrine of the Lord's Supper so strictly. And it should not surprise us that Luther felt that the Swiss had a different spirit than the Lutherans.[20]

> But there was a great dilemma. Various Protestant groups believed that they alone possessed the truth because they interpreted Scripture under the Holy Spirit's illumination, but they had little criteria to work with to distinguish between true and false certainty.[21]

> Chemnitz's answer to the "Protestant dilemma" is plagued by the same problem of circularity as Luther's.[22]

Following that, Bergman delves into an entirely different aspect of certainty as well, as noted previously:

> Chemnitz is willing to minimize the quality of faith, to undermine his scriptural definition of faith as assurance, for the sake of a pastoral need. With such a concession, he comes close to medieval pastoral theologians who also relied on minimization to prevent despair. . . The purpose of the Word. . . is to confer Christ's grace and provide certainty of salvation. According to Chemnitz, indubitable certainty of salvation presupposes that Christians can distinguish true faith from false faith.[23]

> If a Christian cannot have indubitable certainty that their faith is genuine, they cannot have indubitable certainty of justification

---

20. Bergman, "Certainty of Salvation," 77.
21. Bergman, "Certainty of Salvation," 49.
22. Bergman, "Certainty of Salvation," 159.
23. Bergman, "Certainty of Salvation," 239.

and predestination. This conditioning of the knowledge of salvation by one's works is one of the most significant weak points in Chemnitz's position on the indubitable certitude of salvation. After all the arguments for the exclusion of works from justification to guarantee the certainty of salvation, he brings works back through the backdoor to condition the certitude of salvation.[24]

During the past few centuries, it has become less common for Lutherans to insist on the indubitability of the certainty of salvation.[25]

The indubitability of human assurance presumably reflects the post-17th century intellectual development on the unreliability or limited nature of human knowledge. As we noted earlier, in the 16th century, everyone was still convinced that human beings may have infallible religious certainty. In our current context, however, such optimism concerning human knowledge seems unwarranted for many.[26]

Chemnitz's teaching on the certainty of salvation does not warrant indubitable certainty.[27]

To attain absolute certainty regarding your salvation, you must know that you possess true faith. You must also know that your faith has not been demonic faith all along. Ultimately, only Jesus holds the knowledge of this truth and will reveal the reality of our faith on the final day of reckoning. Furthermore, it is essential to be convinced that you hold the singular, authentic interpretation of Scripture while dismissing the teachings of over thirty-five thousand Protestant denominations as misleading or even demonic in nature. As Bergman astutely observes, you lack any definitive criteria—aside from the teachings imparted by your specific denomination and its pastors—to ascertain whether you and your community have genuinely "interpreted Scripture under the illumination of the Holy Spirit."[28]

To satisfy those exacting criteria, one would need to become the polar opposite of a humble Christian, instead embodying the essence of a prideful, self-righteous Pharisee. Furthermore, it would necessitate the creation of a complex facade constructed from a tangle of extraordinary yet unverifiable fabrications, intertwined with deliberate misinterpretations

---

24. Bergman, "Certainty of Salvation," 241.
25. Bergman, "Certainty of Salvation," 243.
26. Bergman, "Certainty of Salvation," 244.
27. Bergman, "Certainty of Salvation," 244.
28. Bergman, "Certainty of Salvation," 49.

of Scripture. This elaborate charade would mask the absence of genuine humility, replacing it with ostentatious displays of self-importance and an air of superiority designed to deceive not only others but oneself as well.

How did the self-deceived Jehovah's Witnesses, the most blatantly gnostic religious group in America, come to believe they had achieved absolute certainty of salvation? It might surprise you to learn that, despite being deeply trapped in a web of deception, their grasp of the fundamental nature of the above issues surpasses that of dispensationalists and mainstream Christians. A profound understanding fuels their unwavering loyalty to the intricate fabrications they have come to believe. The web of interconnected lies provided by the Watchtower organization has skillfully equipped each member with the tools to affirmatively address these essential requisites, fostering a deep sense of conviction that binds them to their beliefs. How were they able to validate these seemingly unconfirmable criteria and, in doing so, ensure that no detail was overlooked in addressing the issues mentioned above?

Firstly, the Jehovah's Witnesses organization skillfully indoctrinated its followers, instilling in them a fervent belief that they alone possess the true interpretation of Scripture. This conviction has fortified their certainty that they alone will be in the kingdom, rendering them impervious to doubt. With unwavering boldness, they insist that all other professed Christians are misled, ensnared in the clutches of the devil, and working tirelessly against "Jehovah's one true church" on Satan's behalf.

They confidently assert that they possess the sole correct interpretation of Scripture, believing wholeheartedly that Jesus Christ himself has been guiding their organization since 1919, articulating and shaping his ever-changing theology through them. However, one could argue that this very assertion should prompt them to reconsider the origins of their theology. Since Jesus Christ, by nature, remains constant and unchanging, then it raises the question of whether their purported "new light," which is what they call the changes God has made, truly stems from him.[29] It seems evident that the changes and updates they receive may originate from some other source entirely.

They hold a steadfast belief that their faith is authentic, deeply rooted in the conviction that their governing body is synonymous with Jehovah God. Because they are constantly faced with the challenge of proving their faith in their authority figures, they are well aware that their trust in the

---

29. Nuccio, "55 Loaded Language Terms."

governing body is authentic, which is undeniable even to outsiders. However, they mistakenly equate this trust with having true faith in God. This blending of beliefs creates a profound sense of spiritual certainty within the community. It not only addresses authentic faith but also cleverly tackles the issue of demonic faith, as Jesus Christ, by heading their organization, can sort that out now through their leadership instead of waiting until the last day.

Ultimately, it becomes clear that the Jehovah's Witnesses possess the extraordinary and unique fabricated capacity to check off all the boxes demanded of Luther and Bergman in order to have certainty of salvation. Only their interpretation of Scripture is true, while other interpretations are from the devil. Only they worship God, while everyone else worships Satan. Only their unwavering loyalty to men, their governing body, qualifies as genuine faith in God. Perfect!

Unfortunately, as everyone reading this can see, the same overwhelming self-righteousness, pride, and self-aggrandizing arrogance of the Jehovah's Witnesses—modern-day Pharisees—that makes them believe they are saved, makes them a gnostic cult. Their self-perceived guarantee of salvation is a complete fraud and a self-delusion.

What could compel a person to plunge headlong into such profound self-deception? A significant part of the answer lies in the alluring mindset they readily embrace. As A. W. Tozer aptly states, "We accept the Christianity of our group as being identical with Christ and his apostles. The beliefs, practices, ethics, [and] activities of our group are equated with the Christianity of the New Testament. Whatever the group thinks or says or does is scriptural, no questions asked. Busying ourselves with the activities of the group [is] keeping the commandments of Christ."[30] While this statement captures a fundamental truth, it still fails to address the deeper question of why individuals become so deeply entrenched in this delusion with such unquestioning fervor.

As Jehovah's Witnesses set out on their door-to-door campaigns, they begin with a tantalizing proposition: "Would you like to live forever in a paradise on earth?" This invitation, rich with enticing imagery, conceals a deeper implication—that they possess the authority to grant salvation itself. The only requirement placed upon potential followers is an unwavering commitment to their tightly knit community. It is this spurious promise of eternal salvation that lures hopeful seekers into willing conformity.

---

30. Tozer, *Best of A. W. Tozer*, 90.

UNACCEPTABLE DIVERGENCE

Once individuals accept the premise that this group holds the keys to their eternal home, their assurance of salvation becomes irrevocably intertwined with their willingness to embrace every tenet presented to them; they are essentially inseparable. The wheels are now greased for the steamroller of indoctrination that follows.

The implausibility of what they're being told hardly registers as their minds have gone blank and "holy emotions" have taken control. The act of surrendering their critical faculties and embracing blind faith intertwines with their very identity, forming an inseparable bond that drives their devotion. In this delicate dance between hope and submission, the allure of a promised paradise feeds an insatiable hunger for certainty that ultimately overrides the instinct to question.

Similarly, virtually every Protestant invitation begins with the same tantalizing guarantee of salvation, which, at least to some extent, influences our willingness to accept their message. This highlights the reality that the present-day American landscape has devolved into a staggering array of thirty-five thousand distinct groups, each vying for our allegiance. When we engage with a particular group, we unwittingly concede their claimed right to bestow salvation upon their followers. We select the one that resonates with us, reflecting our personal preferences and preconceived beliefs: there truly is a church to suit every taste. Remarkably, no prior biblical knowledge is required; the only prerequisite is an unwavering commitment to their beliefs and practices. Every choice we make carries significant eternal weight, often made with nothing more than faith in those who claim to have authority, all of whom uniformly frame it as faith in God. Virtually every one of these groups—whether it's the Jehovah's Witnesses, Mormons, dispensationalists, or your local mainstream Protestant church—assert their authority to dispense salvation.

Everything in the preceding few paragraphs is unmistakably clear when we examine the practices and beliefs of Jehovah's Witnesses. Yet, paradoxically, this same clarity seems to dissipate when we turn the lens inward to evaluate our own lives and the churches we belong to, becoming increasingly nebulous. An earnest introspection, however, may very well validate the assertion made by Philip Lee in an earlier chapter: "Gnostic cults are but caricatures of the more subtle Gnosticism within the Protestant Church itself."[31]

---

31. Lee, *Against the Protestant Gnostics*, 159.

FAKE SALVATION IN MODERN GNOSTIC AMERICA

If you recognize even a tiny part of yourself or your church in their self-serving spiritual methodology and the resultant conviction of the salvific validity of their particular gnostic system, rest assured that you are not alone. Each of us has been shaped and spiritually influenced by the fervent promotion of various aspects introduced by the religious innovators of nineteenth-century America. The intricately crafted and skillfully marketed systems have left an indelible mark on all of modern American Christianity.

As has been exhaustively reinforced throughout this book, all Protestant guarantees of salvation are as valid as the Jehovah's Witness guarantee of salvation, the Mormon guarantee of salvation, or anyone's guarantee of salvation, which means they all are entirely worthless. Every group is acutely aware of Bergman's post-seventeenth-century "unreliability or limited nature of human knowledge"[32] when looking at other groups who falsely guarantee salvation to their members. In a world of approximately 2.5 billion professed Christians,[33] there is a collective acknowledgment that, apart from the relatively few who share our own beliefs, the vast majority are ensnared in deception. Yet, when we turn our gaze inward to assess our own group, we somehow time travel back to the "16th century, [where] everyone was still convinced that human beings may have infallible religious certainty."[34]

This cognitive dissonance exposes a fascinating juxtaposition between our awareness of human fallibility and the unwavering conviction we often harbor in the validity of our own perspectives. While we critique the self-deceived sixteenth-century certainties of others, we remain blissfully unaware of the same vulnerabilities festering within our own ranks. It's apparent that they've been fed falsehoods regarding the assurance of their salvation while we have been enlightened with the truth about ours. The distinction is strikingly clear: we belong to the right gnostic group.

Regrettably, the concept of a right group—be it gnostic or any other type—remains a tantalizing mirage. As countless voices have echoed, the journey to salvation resembles a turnstile, where each individual must pass through alone, one at a time.

All systems that guarantee the members of their group salvation are working from the gnostic script: "The Gnostic texts were written so that

---

32. Bergman, "Certainty of Salvation," 244.
33. Zurlo, "World Christianity."
34. Bergman, "Certainty of Salvation," 244.

the Gnostics could know [the certainty of] their own salvation."[35] That is the entire purpose and emphasis of gnostic systems, as has been covered in detail throughout this book, and the same purpose and emphasis is evident in virtually every modern Protestant church. All of them have adopted concepts from the unique American religious innovators of the past two hundred years.

Steve Gregg concludes his article by saying, "Darby's 'rediscovered truths' [are] a departure from historic Christian theology. [Which means that] either all the Christian scholars prior to 1830 have been wrong about the central teachings of the New Testament, or else the dispensationalists are wrong."[36]

Once again, I find myself reiterating a central argument that I have been developing throughout this entire book. We are faced with a critical question: Have the countless qualified theologians who have devoted themselves to the study of Scripture over the last two millennia been utterly incompetent in their interpretations? If that's the case, do the views of John Nelson Darby, much like a modern-day prophet, truly reflect the singular and authoritative voice of revealed Scripture? Steve Gregg, in his insightful analysis, argues that dispensationalists are misguided in their unquestioning and biblically unfounded adherence to the teachings of Darby—a young man who, at just nineteen, was too impatient to learn Christian history and theology from his college professors and instead took a shortcut and created a series of ideas from his own head.

Throughout the decades, in countless conversations with Jehovah's Witnesses, I have posed a provocative question: Are you truly willing to face an eternity in the depths of hell due to your unwavering faith in a nineteen-year-old egotist, Charles Russell, rather than merely considering the prior two thousand years of biblical history and theology, thereby uncovering the glaring contradictions in what you've been indoctrinated into? Unfortunately, the Watchtower organization's teaching of annihilationism renders my argument moot; if there is no hell, there's no fear of eternal punishment.

I now ask the millions upon millions of American evangelical Christians, mainstream Christians, and those influenced by this pervasive contemporary theology the same provocative question: Are you truly willing to face an eternity in the depths of hell due to your unwavering faith in a

---

35. Lee, *Against the Protestant Gnostics*, 4.
36. Gregg, "Is Dispensationalism Indispensable?"

nineteen-year-old egotist, John Nelson Darby, rather than merely considering the prior two thousand years of biblical history and theology, and some of the points in this book, thereby uncovering the glaring contradictions in what you've been indoctrinated into?

Please take a moment to reflect once more on this Michael LeMay quote: "Something we believe to be true can actually have a contradiction when we learn new information. At that point, we find out if we are humble or proud. If we discover a contradiction in our belief, and we are humble, we change our mind about the belief. But if we choose to ignore the contradiction and choose to believe something that has been proven to be contradictory, we are prideful, and we damage our brains in the long run."[37]

It is my heartfelt hope and earnest prayer that this book may serve as a catalyst for you. May it inspire you to step off the escalator to HELL—a descent that, unbeknownst to many of us, we have been riding together due to the unbiblical teachings and seductive allure of *fake salvation* in *modern gnostic America*.

---

37. LeMay, *Death of Christian Thought*, 70.

BIBLIOGRAPHY

Armstrong, Karen. *A History of God: The 4,000-Year Quest of Judaism, Christianity and Islam*. New York: Ballantine, 2011.
Barnstone, Willis. *The Other Bible*. New York: HarperCollins, 2005.
BBC. "Christadelphians." June 25, 2009. https://www.bbc.co.uk/religion/religions/christianity/subdivisions/christadelphians_1.shtml.
Beautiful Feet. "1541 John Calvin and the Geneva Switzerland Reformation." https://romans1015.com/calvin/.
Bergman, Andreas. "The Certainty of Salvation in the Theology of Martin Chemnitz." PhD diss., University of Helsinki, 2023. https://helda.helsinki.fi/server/api/core/bitstreams/7c6bdf1c-9a13-4dcd-b806-c8510ee621c0/content.
Boer, Paul. *St. Ignatius of Antioch: The Epistles*. North Charleston, SC: CreateSpace, 2012.
Bonhoeffer, Dietrich. *The Cost of Discipleship*. Translated by R. H. Fuller. Revised by Irmgard Booth. New York: Touchstone, 1995.
Bredenhof, Wes. "John Calvin and Michel Servetus." Wes Bredenhof (blog), Feb. 18, 2014. https://bredenhof.ca/2014/02/18/john-calvin-and-michael-servetus/.
Carranza, Christopher Raoul. *The Battle for the Divinity of Christ in the Early Centuries*. Eugene, OR: Resource, 2003.
———. "The Jehovah's Witnesses: Are They the One True Church?" Apr. 5, 2024. Video, 53:09. https://www.youtube.com/watch?v=pWnliPYCQm4.
———. "The Jehovah's Witnesses: Some Timely Truth." Apr. 26, 2024. Video, 22:10. https://www.youtube.com/watch?v=rOusBMwjqbg.
Cary, Phillip. *The History of Christian Theology: Transcript Book*. Guidebook and course transcript, 36 lectures. Great Courses. Chantilly, VA: Teaching Company, 2008.
Chafer, Lewis Sperry, and Walvoord John. *Major Bible Themes*. Rev. ed. Grand Rapids: Zondervan, 1975.
Damick, Andrew Stephen. *Orthodoxy and Heterodoxy*. Chesterton, IN: Ancient Faith, 2017.
Damrosch, Leo. "The Breakup of the Empire." Lecture 16 in *Books That Matter: The History of the Decline and Fall of the Roman Empire*, disc 3. 4 discs. DVD. Great Courses. Chantilly, VA: Teaching Company, 2017.
Dattani, Saloni. "Measuring the Black Death." Asimov Press. https://press.asimov.com/articles/black-death.
DeMar, Gary. "What Jehovah's Witnesses and Last Days Advocates Have in Common." American Vision, June 9, 2022. https://americanvision.org/posts/what-jehovah-s-witnesses-and-last-days-advocates-have-in-common/.

BIBLIOGRAPHY

Eberstadt, Mary. *How the West Really Lost God*. Conshohocken, PA: Templeton, 2014.

Encyclopedia Britannica. "Johann Agricola." Last updated Feb. 25, 2025. https://www.britannica.com/biography/Johann-Agricola.

Eyeons, Keith. "Retreat and Restructuring: Karl Barth's Strategic Use of John's Gospel in the Church Dogmatics." PhD diss., Downing College, 2009.

Farrell, Jenny. "Thomas Müntzer and the German Peasants' War." Culture Matters, May 30, 2025. https://www.culturematters.org.uk/thomas-muntzer-and-the-german-peasants-war/.

Franz, Raymond. *Crisis of Conscience*. 4th ed. Atlanta: Commentary, 2004.

Gagliardi, Juliette. "Number of New Coronavirus (COVID-19) Deaths in Europe Since February 2020." Statista, Dec. 9, 2024. https://www.statista.com/statistics/1102288/coronavirus-deaths-development-europe/.

Galan, Hector, dir. "From Apocalypse to Heresies." Season 1, episode 4 of *Ancient Roads from Christ to Constantine*, disc 2, lect. 1. Featuring Jonathan Phillips. 2 discs. Austin, TX: Galan Productions, 2015.

Gay, Peter. *The Enlightenment: The Rise of Modern Paganism*. New York: Norton, 1977.

Gentry, Kenneth L. "Assurance and Lordship Salvation: The Dispensational Concern." *Dispensationalism in Transition* 6.9 (1993) 1–2. https://www.garynorth.com/freebooks/docs/a_pdfs/newslet/dt/9309.pdf.

Gerstner, John H. *Wrongly Dividing the Word of Truth: A Critique of Dispensationalism*. 3rd ed. Draper, VA: Nicene Council, 2009.

Gregg, Steve. *All You Want to Know About Hell*. Nashville, TN: Nelson, 2013.

———. "Is Dispensationalism Indispensable?" Christian Research Institute, last updated Jan. 31, 2025. https://www.equip.org/articles/dispensationalism-indispensable/.

Houtz, Wyatt. "Martin Luther's Share of the Guilt: Was the Protestant Reformation Really Worth It?" Post Barthian, Oct. 29, 2017. https://postbarthian.com/2017/10/29/martin-luthers-share-guilt-protestant-reformation-really-worth/.

Hunt, Dave. *What Love Is This?* Sisters, OR: Loyal, 2002.

Idleman, Kyle. *Not a Fan: Becoming a Completely Committed Follower of Jesus*. Grand Rapids: Zondervan, 2009.

Lee, Philip J. *Against the Protestant Gnostics*. New York: Oxford University Press, 1987.

LeMay, Michael D. *The Death of Christian Thought*. Abbotsford, WI: Aneko, 2016.

Ligonier Editorial. "What Are Legalism and Antinomianism?" Ligonier Ministries, Apr. 5, 2023. https://learn.ligonier.org/articles/field-guide-on-false-teaching-legalism-antinomianism.

Ligonier Ministries. "The Clarity of Scripture: Deuteronomy 6:6–9." Feb. 13, 2017. https://learn.ligonier.org/devotionals/clarity-scripture.

Luther, Martin. "A Treatise Against Antinomians Written in an Epistolary Way." True Covenanter, last updated Apr. 29, 2025. https://www.truecovenanter.com/truelutheran/luther_against_the_antinomians.html.

MacCulloch, Diarmaid. *All Things Made New: The Reformation and Its Legacy*. Grand Haven, MI: Brilliance Audio, Apr. 25, 2017. Audible audio ed., 17 hr., 50 min.

Mark, Joshua J. "Religious Responses to the Black Death." World History Encyclopedia, Apr. 16, 2020. https://www.worldhistory.org/article/1541/religious-responses-to-the-black-death/.

"Martin Luther's Anfechtungen—His Own Dark Nights of the Soul, and How They Affected His Teaching and Ministry." Grateful to the Dead, Aug. 24, 2011. https://

BIBLIOGRAPHY

gratefultothedead.com/2011/08/24/martin-luthers-anfechtungen-his-own-dark-nights-of-the-soul-and-how-they-affected-his-teaching-and-ministry/.

Martin, Walter. *Kingdom of the Cults*. Minneapolis, MN: Bethany House, 1965.

McLeod, Hugh. *The Religious Crisis of the 1960s*. Reprint. Oxford: Oxford University Press, 2013.

Mohler, Albert. "'The Rise and Fall of Dispensationalism'—A Conversation with Daniel Hummel About Dispensationalism in America and in the Evangelical Mind." Albert Mohler (website), Aug. 23, 2023. https://albertmohler.com/2023/08/23/daniel-hummel/.

Monticello. "Jefferson's Religious Beliefs." Aug. 2012. https://www.monticello.org/research-education/thomas-jefferson-encyclopedia/jeffersons-religious-beliefs/.

Nuccio, Sylviane. "55 Loaded Language Terms Only Jehovah's Witnesses Use and Understand." Medium, Jan. 12, 2018. https://medium.com/@SylvianeNuccio/55-loaded-language-terms-only-jehovahs-witnesses-use-and-understand-2e89e8a906dd.

Pietz, Tim. "Antinomianism: The Heresy You Never Knew You Had." Crosswalk, last updated Dec. 22, 2020. https://www.crosswalk.com/faith/spiritual-life/what-is-antinomianism.html.

Rhodes, Ron. "Jehovah's Witnesses and the Doctrine of Salvation." ATRI, May 14, 2024. https://blog.atriresearch.org/articles/jehovahs-witnesses-and-the-doctrine-of-salvation.

Roper, Lyndal. "The German Peasants' War, 1524–1525." University of Oxford, Mar. 30, 2021. https://www.history.ox.ac.uk/article/the-german-peasants-war-15241525.

Rose, Devon. *The Protestant's Dilemma*. El Cajon, CA: Catholic Answers, 2014.

Russell, Charles Taze. *Thy Kingdom Come*. New York: Watch Tower Society, 1891.

Ryrie, Charles. *Balancing the Christian Life*. Chicago: Moody, 1969.

Schooping, Joshua. *Disillusioned*. Russellville, AR: Theophany, 2023.

Scorah, Amber. "Leaving the Witness." *Believer*, Feb. 1, 2013. https://www.thebeliever.net/leaving-the-witness/.

Sickafoose, Munro. "Four Hundred and Sixty-Three." Sermon transcript, delivered at the Unitarian Congregation of Taos, Dec. 15, 2019. https://uutaos.org/wp-content/uploads/2019/12/FourHundres63-UCOT-12-15-19-.pdf.

Sobolewski, Adrian. "The Polish Brethren: The First Reformed Peace Church and Poland's First Banned Religion." Culture.pl, last updated Sept. 10, 2021. https://culture.pl/en/article/the-polish-brethren-the-first-reformed-peace-church-polands-first-banned-religion.

Steyn, Mark. *America Alone: The End of the World as We Know It*. Washington, DC: Regnery, 2006.

Szkuta, Magda. "Arians in the Age of the Polish Reformation." European Studies (blog), Feb. 2, 2018. https://blogs.bl.uk/european/2018/02/arians-in-the-age-of-the-polish-reformation.html.

Tozer, A. W. *The Best of A. W. Tozer*. Edited by Warren W. Wiersbe. Harrisburg, PA: Baker, 1978.

———. *The Knowledge of the Holy*. New York: Harper Collins, 1961.

———. *Man: The Dwelling Place of God*. San Antonio, TX: Bibliotech, 2016.

———. *The Pursuit of God*. Mansfield Center, CT: Martino, 2009.

———. *The Radical Cross*. Chicago: Moody, 2015.

BIBLIOGRAPHY

Watchtower Society. "Seventy Years' Desolation (Part II)." *Watchtower*, June 15, 1922. https://jws-library.one/?file=data/1922/w_E_19220615/w_E_19220615.html.

———. "What Is Needed for Salvation?" *Watchtower*, Dec. 1, 1967, 707–11. https://wol.jw.org/en/wol/d/r1/lp-e/1967880.

Wikipedia. "Christianity in the 19th Century." Wikimedia Foundation, last updated May 7, 2025. https://en.wikipedia.org/wiki/Christianity_in_the_19th_century.

———. "Jehovah's Witnesses and Salvation." Wikimedia Foundation, last updated May 19, 2025. https://en.wikipedia.org/wiki/Jehovah%27s_Witnesses_and_salvation.

———. "Nelson H. Barbour." Wikimedia Foundation, last updated April 9, 2024. https://en.wikipedia.org/wiki/Nelson_H._Barbour.

Wilson, Eric. "Remembering Carl Olof Jonsson." Beroean Pickets, Apr. 17, 2023. https://beroeans.net/2023/04/17/carl-jonsson.

———. *Shutting the Door to the Kingdom of God: How the Watchtower Stole Salvation from Jehovah's Witnesses*. Willington, DE: Good News Association, 2022.

Zurlo, Gina. "World Christianity: It's Annual Statistical Table Time!" Overseas Ministries Study Center. https://omsc.ptsem.edu/world-christianity-its-annual-statistical-table-time/.

www.ingramcontent.com/pod-product-compliance
Lightning Source LLC
Chambersburg PA
CBHW072144160426
43197CB00012B/2243